Toward
Curriculum
for
Being

SUNY Series, Curriculum Issues and Inquiries
Edmund C. Short, Editor

TOWARD CURRICULUM FOR BEING

Voices of Educators

Louise M. Berman
Francine H. Hultgren
Diane Lee
Mary S. Rivkin
Jessie A. Roderick
in Conversation with Ted Aoki

Foreword by Catharine R. Stimpson

STATE UNIVERSITY OF NEW YORK PRESS

Production by Dana Foote
Marketing by Dana E. Yanulavich

Published by
State University of New York Press, Albany

© 1991 State University of New York

For information, address State University of New York
Press, State University Plaza, Albany, N.Y., 12246

Library of Congress Cataloging in Publication Data

Toward Curriculum for Being: Voices of Educators / Louise M. Berman
   [et al.]; in Conversation with Ted Aoki
       p.   cm. — (SUNY series, curriculum issues and inquiries)
     Includes bibliographical references.
       ISBN 0–7914–0630–X (alk. paper). — ISBN 0–7914–0631–8 (pbk. :
   alk. paper)
       1. Teaching.   2. Education—United States—Curricula.
   3. Ontology.   4. Education—United States—Philosophy.
   5. Educators—United States—Attitudes.   I. Berman, Louise M.
   II. Aoki, Ted T.   III. Series: SUNY series in curriculum issues and
   inquiries.
   LB1025.2.T69   1991
   375′ .00973—dc20   90–40121
                                                                          CIP

10 9 8 7 6 5 4 3 2 1

Contents

Foreword

"I dwell," wrote Emily Dickinson in Poem 657, "in Possibility—A fairer House than Prose." Over a century later, the authors of *Toward Curriculum for Being: Voices of Educators* are renovating and extending Dickinson's home. Candidly, wholeheartedly, they have committed themselves to the possibility of the renewal of education.

The birth of *Toward Curriculum for Being* is itself a story of renewal. A few years ago, seven women educators in the Washington, DC, area who were interested in teacher training formed a study group. It was at once a seminar, conversation, and self-designed course in survival skills. The women were balancing the demands of job and family, but remarkably, they found the energy to cook for each other. Literally and figuratively, they nourished each other. They had to balance hope and dismay as well. For they were passionately committed to teaching and learning, to educating—educating themselves, each other, the student teachers in their college classrooms, the children in any classroom. Yet they were also alienated from educational systems that preferred technology to humanity and from educational research that deployed a rigid scientism instead of supple readings of reality.

The women read reality together, especially through work in phenomenology, hermeneutics, and radical theories of pedagogy. They analyzed knowledge as a social construct; knowing as an act of inquiry and interpretation; language as the matrix of meaning; and the using of language, especially metaphor, as our human way of creating meaning. They studied the ethics of care, our obligation to attend to and tend each other's needs. They talked and listened to each other, moving among their own personal stories, scrutinies of education, and perceptions of the world-at-large. Conscious of feminism, they were aware of the importance of women choosing to speak by and for themselves. If such speech often seems initially hesitant, it is not a sign of a faltering, halting mind but of a woman carefully picking her way through a landscape in upheaval. The group also began to present papers at academic conferences. If their study group was an example of another kind of classroom, a classroom that is a vital community, their panels were examples of another way of doing and sharing research, one which abhorred the jargon of a reductive positivism without a human face.

Now five of these women—Diane, Francine, Jessie, Louise, and Mary—have created *Toward Curriculum for Being.* From time to time, a sixth voice, that of Ted, speaks with them. In order to hold these six voices, the book must mingle several genres: autobiography, group history, educational theory, philosophical inquiry, and visionary Utopianism, which calls on us to believe that our world can be different from and better than it is. Or, as Dickinson writes rather more vividly in Poem 657, we spread wide our "narrow Hands / To gather Paradise—". Each voice, however, speaks to a common set of themes. Each insists on the significance of the person, the whole individual, in the classroom. Teachers, who must be pupils as well, and students, who are teachers as well, together embark upon the journey of education with an open, not closed, end.

In brief, education is a quest, a series of turns, returns, and detours, not a forced march, not a series of tests, pretests, and measurements of the acquisition of skills. A teacher is neither technocrat, autocrat, nor bureaucrat, but a pilgrim. *Curriculum* is not a fixed, predetermined body of knowledge, but a metaphor. As metaphor, it stands for at least three phenomena: first, the structures within which, through which, and beyond which we recognize each other's being; next, the dialog teachers and students have with each other during the process of education; and finally, an "inheritance," a legacy of human achievement and ruthlessness, the record that one generation passes down to the next for it to play or break.

In *Toward Curriculum for Being,* Mary, who teaches science education to preschool teachers, speaks movingly of the inheritance of science, the "conceived world that the teacher seeks to bring to the student." She loves science, but modern scientific practices frighten her. To her relief, she has found that such feminist thinkers as Evelyn Fox Keller and Dorothy Smith give her some hope for change in these practices. I admit that I read Mary's sections with particular attention, for she is my blood sister. With her I shared infancy, childhood, adolescence, and now, some post-modern maturity. But who, I wondered, is she as an educator? Her references to growing up in a "large, close family" in the Pacific Northwest startled me into an only partly nostalgic, unspoken dialog. We were competitive as well as close, I muttered, jealous as well as mutually protective. Why, I growled on, are you reading only European philosophers? Where is Dewey? James? Rorty? But, I said, more generously, our big and varied family *was* a crackling model school. We learned from a father who taught astronomy by tracing the Big Dipper during cookouts on a summer night; a mother who taught literature by reading poetry aloud night after night; a grandfather who taught arithmetic by playing round after round of cribbage and rummy.

So schooled, my sister says: "I reflect on these teaching times...
and... appreciate the observation that what you actually teach is yourself... I do not completely understand this text I teach but there seem
to be some irreducibles: an elemental belief in freedom, a desire for
grace, and a yearning for community" (p. 67). Freedom, grace, community—these are my values, too, reflected in all the curious, courageous
voices in *Toward Curriculum for Being* who weave and reweave human value into the thick tapestries of education.

Catharine R. Stimpson
University Professor and Dean of
the Graduate School
Rutgers University

Preface

"Education is Being." So announced a banner mounted outside the Institute for Education of the University of Heidelberg, Germany, where this past summer some educators assembled in conference. On seeing this banner, a non-educator friend from Montreal, Canada, excitedly informed me. Without doubt she would have received a resounding response from the authors of *Toward Curriculum for Being: Voices of Educators.*

I like to think it was no happenstance that, at the moment I received word from my friend, I was engrossed in Milan Kundera's *The Art of the Novel.* In it, Kundera, remembering Heidegger's deep concern, speaks seriously of how contemporary novelists and storytellers should address the forgetfulness of 'being' in the Western world. I nodded with him in agreement as he wrote of how narrative inquiry of lived experiences can disclose the existential texture of the beings we have come to be.

In a like sense, the five educator-authors of this book are deeply concerned by the way in which so many educators in North America, including themselves, have generally become enamored of scientism and instrumentalism, in the wake of which they seem to have become inured to the texture of the half-life of who they might be as educators. No doubt it is a deep concern for the erosion of educators' personhood that prompted a committed group of thoughtful educators at the University of Maryland to gather in frequent conversations over several years, a remarkable feat in itself. In the midst of their own teaching experiences at the university level, these educators opened themselves to a question that insistently called upon them from the ground of their own vocation—that mode of being called curriculum as experienced.

Readers will find in *Toward Curriculum for Being: Voices of Educators* animated reflections on ontological interests of these educators, beckoning them to listen to their unique journeys. Persons will be drawn into the authors' varied turnings and re-turnings as they, in the midst of their coursings, compose enchanting discourses.

I was invited to the threshold of this small but vigorous community into which thoughtful conversations of a year or so had wrought. Committed to action research geared to their own pedagogic and curricular experiences, they opened themselves to me to enter into their ongoing flow of conversations and writings that had already culminated in an AERA symposium: "Curriculum Inquiry as Being: Reflections of a Study Group Encountering Each Other through Interpretive Inquiry."

It was exhilarating to join a group of educators bent on exploring what it is to be interpretive researchers by searching and re-searching into their own personal curricular and pedagogical experiences within their own university setting. It was exciting to be allowed into an ambience of hermeneutic quest given to enhancing their understanding of their own effort to ontological disclosure appropriated within a conversational setting.

Already engaged in an effort to understand human conversation not so much as something they themselves conduct but more so as something they fall into and in-dwell within, as Hans-Georg Gadamer suggested, the five educators seemed to sense that, in truth, they in conversation are being led by the phenomenon that called them together in the first place. They seemed to be inspirited by surrendering to the conversation's own spirit.

So inspired, they appeared to acknowledge the mutuality of questions and answers of which Gadamer speaks. Bowing to such mutuality, they acknowledged that at times their writings and speakings were already answers to questions which at times they held unconsciously. In such situations, they beckoned questions to come into presence, simultaneously coming to a deeper sense of the interplay between questions and answers. They seemed to be attuned to the call of the questions which, even unseen or unheard, seemed to guide their search for understanding. In other words, they acknowledged the hermeneutical priority of the question which was the central feature of the AERA symposium, "Conversations across Disciplines: Hermeneutic Priority of the Question for the Interpretation of Curriculum Text."

Many of the questions concerning meanings of personal experience took the format of "What is it *like* to be ...?" Our educator-authors became alertly conscious of how often, in unfolding meaning, poetic metaphors issue revealingly from human groundedness in humus. A profound respect for metaphorical discourse became increasingly patent as readers will find in the papers presented at the symposium entitled "Revealing the Meaning of Metaphors that Guide Curricular Practice: Speaking, Reflecting, Writing."

Toward Curriculum for Being: Voices of Educators deserves this final comment. Throughout the year-by-year venture, the five educators in their hermeneutic effort insistently tried to open themselves to the realm beyond generalizable, conceptual, and abstractive knowings. Readers will find in these writings the educators' search for embodied knowings that disclose insights that generalized knowings are unable to offer. With such interest, their discourse frequently relied on images that depend on sightings of the eye (note the reliance on metaphors reflecting insights, images, visions, envisionings, and illuminations. But over these years, increasingly we find discourse that pertains to the ear, reflected in wordings such as *listening to callings, seeking attunement,* and *finding resonance.* Increasingly, their discourse reflects both the world of sight and the world of sound.

On this point, I proffer a thought. With these educators' increasing attunement to "personhood" as a highlighted notion, the priority of their allegiance to the eye diminished and is complemented by an allegiance to the notion of sound. Could it be that in their search for the original ground of being, they found resonance with the original etymological understanding of *person* as *per* [through] + *sonare* [to sound]? Such a view is somewhat reminiscent of late Wittgenstein, who in his own turnings began to question Modernism's fidelity to the primacy of the visual—that which eyes can see. Indeed, the tone of the discourse as being is what readers may find of interest in the later writings of these author-educators.

The book resounds with five voices. How shall we hear these voices? I suggest that readers be mindful of what they hear as they read. In fact, they might be sensitive to the polysonic nature of these voices. For myself, these voices do not blend in a closure; rather, they celebrate openness to openness—there is a distinct resistance on their part to be brought to a closure. I liken these five voices not to a symphonic harmony of oneness, but, as in certain Bach fugues, to a polyphony of five lines in a tensionality of contrapuntal interplay, a tensionality of differences.

Ted Aoki, Professor Emeritus,
The University of Alberta,
Canada

Acknowledgments

Many persons have enriched our lives during our conversations which have culminated in this book. As we talk together we hear the strength, support, and questioning of numerous voices.

The American Educational Research Association (AERA) provided a forum for numerous persons to interact with us. In our initial conversations, Max van Manen offered encouragement and suggestions for engaging in interpretive inquiry. At another session, Mary Ellen Hoy and Emily Slunt shared the table with us and called us to see anew our dialog from the perspectives of education in early childhood and nursing. Likewise, Marian White-Hood shared her perspectives from the stance of home economics.

Our lives are constantly enriched as we continue to be in teaching together. We are also supported by our students, family, and colleagues who remain active participants in our conversations.

We are grateful to a number of persons associated with SUNY Press for their interest and sustained help along the way. Edmund C. Short, Series Editor of Curriculum Issues and Inquiries, listened to our voices as we explored our ideas at AERA meetings. His invitation to consider a book for his series resulted in this volume. The voice of Lois G. Patton, Editor-in-Chief, has provided quiet, supportive direction. Dana Foote, Production Editor, gave thoughtful attention to the unity and coherence of the publication.

Ted Aoki played a major role in the development of this book. Even though he does not sit at our tables in Maryland, he is very much part of our dialog. Ted has never been too busy to help us support our ideas through very thoughtful letters, through participating with us in annual meetings of the American Educational Research Association, through telephone conversations, and through occasional meetings with one of our group. Ted is a Canadian, most recently with distinguished careers at the University of British Columbia and the University of Alberta. Most of all he is a brilliant and compassionate human being with qualities that transcend gender and national boundaries.

We also acknowledge publishers' permission to reprint the following:

Four lines of poetry from Wallace Stevens' "Esthetique du Mal," (p. 125). Copyright 1947 by Wallace Stevens. Reprinted from The Collected Poems of Wallace Stevens, by permission of Alfred A. Knopf, Inc.

With One Voice: An Introduction

This book grew out of a study group which began when one individual invited six persons to join her for an evening to share concerns about research. Six years later, five of the seven persons still gather around dining room tables in one another's homes.* In addition to the original agenda, the group of five educators shares the complexities and intensities of their lives, including their beings as professional persons.

Although the group did not originally set out to write a book, it has and continues to engage in a variety of ventures, some of which culminated in this volume. At the heart of being together is meaning-making as we mull over, discuss, and appropriate insights from texts written by group members and by others. In addition to being in a shared space, we are in teaching together—teaching within an interpretive mode, teaching embedded in an ethic of caring.

As the group met over time, the dialog frequently turned to the meaning of our concerns for curriculum. Early on we identified as a common theme our movement from a logical positivist approach to curriculum and teaching to considering the field within interpretive modes. Our journey together seems to have a rhythm—individual reflection on text, creation and recreation of text, conversations about personal meaning-making and appropriation of common text, and public sharing of individual pilgrimages. Small group conversations, personal reflection, and public discourse all were part of our early group process. We continue to be together in similar ways.

Voices of Educators

The voices you hear in this book are the voices of five experienced educators, all associated with academia. Although each individual has a particular professional arena such as science, home economics, human development, curriculum theory and development, and communication arts, the common interest of the group is a view of curriculum as enhancing being rather than merely imparting knowledge and skills.

The book is organized so that the voice of each educator begins with a brief autobiographical statement followed by two or three papers originally prepared for national conferences of the American Educational Research Association. We have organized the book by persons rather than by topics since our emphasis is upon personhood, upon being. A sixth educator did not participate at our regular meetings because of distance. His voice joined the conversation at two of our AERA sessions and his mode of questioning is continued in this volume.

---

*Jana Staton and Jane White were in the original group.

Our first symposium consisted of papers, collectively titled "Curriculum Inquiry as Being: Reflections of a Study Group Encountering Each Other through Interpretive Inquiry." The second set of papers spoke to the topic "Conversation across Disciplines: Hermeneutical Priority of the Question for the Interpretation of Curriculum Text." Here the focus was upon the potential contribution of Gadamer's concept of the hermeneutic nature of conversation for understanding curriculum. An attempt was made to illuminate the act of hermeneutic questioning. To prepare for this session discussions of individual texts were tape-recorded. The typescripts were then studied for the disclosure of meanings and the emergence of new questions.

The role of metaphor was later considered in terms of its place in interpretive inquiry. Thus a third session focused on "Researching the Meaning of Metaphors that Guide Curricular Practice: Speaking, Reflecting, Writing." Here persons attempted to explore the transformative metaphors that group members created in their own teaching and inquiry.

No effort was made to arrive at a common voice. Rather, this work reflects the yearnings, dilemmas, desires, and questions each individual faces in engaging in dialog around the table. Although the issue continuously surfaces as to whether inquiry into curriculum as being necessitates a new language, the issue has not been resolved. The chapters, however, reflect each person's struggle to frame insights in ways that communicate. At the same time recognition is given to the limitations of certain of our traditional ways of discussing curriculum and curricular inquiry. At points we are tentative. We are trying to present honestly ourselves and our thinking in the context of a complex field.

Our conversations typically take place in our homes. Ordinarily meetings are scheduled in the evenings. Since most of us teach evening classes, we face the persistent task of juggling the meeting schedule so that no person has the regular burden of rushing from class to the home where we gather. During the first few minutes of each meeting, we bring each other up-to-date on the multiple facets of our lives. Persons rejoice in the joys of others and share concerns when one of the group faces a trial. When all arrive, the dining table becomes the gathering place. Although the understanding is that we meet for dessert or snacks, frequently more substantive food appears if a member is known to arrive from teaching or otherwise to have had a long day. Repasts are simple, but ordinarily rather elegantly served on "the good dishes." As the teacups and coffee cups are filled, mounds of papers and books begin to be perched precariously among the dishes and goodies. Persons frequently share books or articles they are currently reading. Written text, tape recordings, and notes are sometimes referred to as the partially preplanned agenda for the evening unfolds. When weariness begins to set in or clock time suggests closure, the discussion moves to a broad shaping of plans for the next meeting, and lengthy farewells are said.

Even as we did not plan to write a book, neither did we plan to network. Yet networking certainly occurs among us. Leadership is shared. It passes from one to another as the various gifts individuals possess are highlighted at appropriate times. Initiating an activity, providing substance for reflection, sharing feelings about turning in a new direction, giving organizational help, supporting a potentially fruitful idea, creating a fresh way of seeing the old, or simply being present to listen—all are gifts which persons present with discernment. All are gifts of being. The search for being, for meaning for self and others, provides the impetus and sustaining power of the group. We are further sustained by our search for forms of curricular practice and inquiry that lead to curricula being. Our searchings and questionings integrate personal and professional lives.

Our Voices in the Context of Others

This work is grounded in the insights of such interpretive theorists as Ted Aoki, Max van Manen, Maxine Greene, Jürgen Habermas, Paul Ricoeur, Hans-Georg Gadamer, Vivian Darroch and Ronald J. Silvers, and Martin Heidegger. References are made to these authors throughout our text. Aoki and van Manen actively entered our struggles as they participated with us in various ways, including AERA sessions. The group began with varying levels of expertise in the works of these authors, but all gained considerable perspective on them during our time together.

Even though slight editorial changes were made in the papers for purposes of clarity, papers appear basically as they were presented. By honoring the original text, we gave priority to representing our being at each moment in time. This conscious choice reflects our commitment to the phenomenological spirit that guided our work—the growth and diversity in our thinking, the record of our journey as it happened, the interdependency of thought revealing the individual in solitude and community, and the social construction of knowledge. Thus Francine's papers are longer as she attempts to illuminate the process from the literature as well as from her personal experience. Another example of diversity in this book is Ted's conversation with

Diane in the form of letters. Furthermore, we all read from different fields, bringing ideas and texts to the tables.

The bases, assumptions, themes, and questions of interpretive theory seem to resonate with our lives as women. We did not set out to deal with women's issues. In fact, men such as Ted Aoki and Max van Manen seemed to share many of our concerns. In retrospect, however, our work frequently echoes themes found in contemporary feminist writing.

Caring was a prominent theme in our writing related to the works of Carol Gilligan (1982), Nell Noddings (1984), Milton Mayeroff (1971), and Martin Heidegger (1962). Caring originates in a reverence for life as Sara Lawrence Lightfoot (1988) describes in the biography of her mother.

Along with that reverence is a respect for wonder, joy, and creativity. We prefer to "dance in Sarah's circle" rather than to "climb Jacob's ladder" (Fox 1979). Our entanglements with life call for concentration, and we are constantly "composing a life," as Mary Catherine Bateson (1989) describes it. We, like Lightfoot's mother, a psychoanalyst, too are gaining fulfillment from balancing the calls of family life and work.

As in *Women of Academe* (Aisenberg and Harrington 1988), we tend to view knowledge contextually, to seek out fields and topics which enrich the interior life, and to deal with topics in a cross-disciplinary way. Thus, frequently we experience marginality both in its goodness and its harshness.

Two of us are raising children, but all of us display the psychological qualities associated with "mothering." We experience the looking, gazing, and watchfulness which Madeline Grumet (1988) discusses in her consideration of women and teaching. We seem to be attuned to seeing, to reflecting, and to trying to understand before leaping.

We listen to stories, and in that process we find our stories to resemble those of other contemporary women writers. As women coming together to create, recreate, and share our life stories, we can constitute a context for listening, learning, and interpreting—a context which may not be present in the larger worlds we inhabit. Support for this endeavor is found in our own experiences, but strength can also be garnered by looking to the efforts of other groups who dialogue for a variety of reasons. One such group is The Personal Narratives Group of academic women, including students, which has found a home in the University of Minnesota Center for Advanced Feminist Studies where its initial activity was a conference in which the group members shared papers on their current research. Dialog emanating from the conference led to the writing of *Interpreting Women's Lives: Feminist Theory and Personal Narratives* (1989), a book which reflects the group's "intellectual struggle to locate useful interpretive frames for women's personal narratives" (p. 12). The group's commitment to grounding feminist theory in women's lives and to viewing women's personal narratives as "essential primary documents for feminist research" (p. 4) has provided the impetus for their work of interpreting text created by themselves and other women.

Toward Curriculum for Being

The themes and issues which emerged from our being together are appropriate for consideration in curriculum development in elementary, secondary, or postsecondary settings. Among the themes we would consider in developing curriculum for being are the following: the person as significant, education as journey, language as meaning, knowledge as constructed, and teacher as pilgrim. Each is briefly discussed here and is considered in more detail in subsequent sections.

Person as Significant

Throughout our discussions, the significance of the person is highlighted. Persons are considered as sacred, holy, whole, thinking, meaning-making, trusting, searching for collegiality and friendship, and questioning. The multiple responsibilities of persons cause them to live in a kind of tension, which draws attention to the importance of wise decision-making. Knowing when to live with one's plans and when to build on the possibilities of the moment necessitates a skill and attunement to self and others.

As educators we resonate with the concepts of caring, of grace, and of tact as important to our continuing desire to be together. Indeed a curriculum of being necessitates an emphasis on the primacy of caring. In many of our discussions we noted the best-laid curriculum plans gone awry when students did not have opportunities to be cared for or to show care.

Education as Journey

In education, we journey together, journey with others who are significant and those who may be more distant from us. The question becomes: In what manner might we journey with others in ways that make the journey meaningful for all? Most of the time our journey is sweet; on occasion the journey presents problems and dilemmas. The concept of detour enters our conversations. Brambles and thickets may cover portions of the path.

In our journey we are aware that we engage in directional planning, but we are not always sure of clear objectives. New questions constantly emerge. Answers give rise to fresh questions. The journey in silence, as well as the journey in voice with others, may be intense, difficult, and all-engrossing. Such feelings are the stuff of life and are handled rather than considered only "soft" or unimportant. Each life is seen as sacred as persons travel side by side.

The journey metaphor helps us fasten on curriculum as nonlinear, as recursive, as geared to the emerging interests of travelers. It helps us see the unforeseen not as something to be ignored or abhorred, but as something to consider as a possibility. In-flight decision making characterizes the travelers.

Language as Meaning

As persons travel, an attempt is made to focus upon the meanings travelers are bringing to the journey. Thus an enthusiastic, indeed a passionate, interest in language guides our thinking and might be central to persons interested in curriculum for being.

Our initial considerations gave attention to the language of research in education. We found certain terms and concepts such as data, control, interviews, and researcher detachment from the process of inquiry incompatible with the perspective of the interpretive inquirer. Instead we wished to talk about uncovering meaning, possibilities, conversations, and the place of the researcher's values in the process of inquiry. A tension existed between the language of research as it is commonly used and the language we perceived to be more attuned to us. A tension also existed for some of us about using a language which communicated to persons of different research persuasions as well as persons who shared our basic orientation. What is the responsibility of persons in sharing their meanings with others? Are we to be like artists who use their gifts to "make a statement" to the outside world, or do we try to ensure that others at least partially understand our sense-making as we move through life.

The above dilemma encountered by our group suggests the nature of certain of the dilemmas which we face relative to language. As persons increasingly make sense out what impinges on their lives, what responsibility do they have to share that sense-making with others? What is the meaning of community within different persuasions of the meaning of language? Each group may deal with these questions as curriculum for specific settings is considered.

The group finds the use of metaphor a profound way to extend our thinking. The metaphors in what follows are too numerous to mention here. We find that the utilization of metaphor frees us to think creatively. Such language helps us extend our sense of reality. Metaphor used in curricular inquiry may help individuals sharpen and extend their thinking. Metaphor helps us probe more deeply and obtain fresher insights.

Knowledge as Personally Constructed

Although the group focuses upon being as the centerpiece of curricular inquiry, considerable attention is given within that orientation to the place of knowledge. In retrospect, we value a process of question-asking, finding answers or partial answers, and then asking other questions based on our answers. We are interested in profundity of thought and are therefore concerned with socially constructed knowledge as opposed to a surface-knowing of "public" knowledge.

The impetus for knowing is seen as coming from the individual in relation to the world. The focus, therefore, of dealing with knowledge is upon what each individual makes of experience rather than on the experience itself. Reflection therefore is critical to knowing.

Persons come to know in community as well as in solitude. Personal sharing of text through dialog and conversation enables new insights to emerge. The gentle, caring, but stimulating community sparks the generation of knowledge and new questions for which answers need to be sought.

Knowledge may be socially constructed in any area. The dichotomy between technical and philosophical knowledge is blurred when the hands and fingertips are seen as extensions of being. Vocational subjects, the arts, nursing, and other areas which have strong "hands-on" components therefore may be seen as socially constructed when persons are encouraged to embed the "hands-on" dimensions within broader meanings. Thus any field may be seen as one in which persons come to know in meaningful ways.

The more persons come to realize the joy and satisfaction that can come from personally constructing knowledge, the greater the sense of aliveness and liveliness. Indeed, persons may come to feel the excitement of life when they free themselves to be totally human.

Teacher as Pilgrim

Earlier the point is made that curriculum for being involves a journey on which pilgrims attempt to make sense of their lives. This sense-making more readily occurs when fellow companions share in the reflective mode, when they are caring, and when they value dialog as a major way of conducting inquiry and generating knowledge. Teachers then are fellow pilgrims—thoughtful professional beings ever reflecting upon their own assumptions and ever dwelling in questions significant to them, even as they encourage students to dwell in their own questions.

A curriculum for being is based on the assumption that teachers are caring, self-motivated, and interested in providing settings for the enhancement of the persons whom they teach. Teaching then is not legislated but comes about through the intensity and care of the conversations among persons striving to become more sensitive and knowing. In lieu of large numbers of persons serving in capacities to centralize the curriculum, teachers tend to have more options for determining the curriculum. After all, the focus is upon being and not only on knowing or doing. Teachers may tend to develop their own networks, their own collaboratives to serve as support systems for themselves. These networks or support groups might be characterized by shared and shifting leadership, voluntary membership, communication about deeply felt needs, and a sense of caring which serve as the glue with little formal structure. Networks are ordinarily ways of being together rather than means to produce products. Products, however, may result from being together.

In the previous few pages we have spoken in one voice as we have reflected on insights we have gained through our being together. Our engagement in the lives of one another continues. We invite you now to listen to each of our individual voices.

References

Aisenberg, N. and M. Harrington (1988). *Women of academe: Outsiders in the sacred grove.* Amherst, MA: The University of Massachusetts Press.

Bateson, M. C. (1989). *Composing a life.* New York: The Atlantic Press.

Fox, M. (1979). *A spirituality named compassion.* Minneapolis: Winston Press.

Gilligan, C. (1982). *In a different voice.* Cambridge, MA: Harvard University Press.

Grumet, M. (1988). *Bitter milk: Women and teaching.* Amherst, MA: The University of Massachusetts Press.

Heidegger, M. (1962). *Being and time.* New York: Harper & Row.

Lightfoot, S. (1988). *Balm in Gilead: Journey of a healer.* Reading, MA: Addison-Wesley.

Mayeroff, M. (1971). *On caring.* New York: Harper & Row.

Noddings, N. (1984). *Caring: A feminine approach to ethics and moral education.* Berkeley: University of California Press.

The Personal Narratives Group (Eds.), (1989). *Interpreting women's lives: Feminist theory and personal narratives.* Bloomington, IN: Indiana University Press.

Francine's Voice

In what manner can I bring my self forward as I attempt to be present through an announcement or revealing of my identity to you? For me the way is through a phenomenological description of my experienced biography.

I am one of them—the first group to be known as baby boomers! *Born in northwestern Minnesota to second-generation Norwegians who both worked as general store proprietors... Father—8th grade education... Mother—one year college and teaching certificate... Brother—age six. Life was good. Family was stable.*

I loved school—that wonderful two-room school! In the "Little Room" (grades 1–3) I learned competition well as the others observed us perform and I excelled. I was also cared for by a loving teacher.... I wanted to be like her. Brother two arrived on the scene while I was in the "Little Room"—a good show and tell!

The "Big Room" (grades 4–6)... less memories here... Stop... Our family now became four... Father died. I lost a portion of my childhood abruptly... Mother gave up her hopes of being a teacher again... Older brother left for college... Younger brother never really knew father... Our family was uprooted... And I became a pedagogue before my time.

High school... More competition... Some academic but more extra-curricular. Music—Band—Choir—Cheerleading—and 4–H events (I still have the purple ribbons). Doing and Making... Where was being? A special home economics teacher... A major chosen... A call to being through making and doing and yes knowing.

The University of Minnesota... A turning... Inward... Quiet reflectivity... Student teaching— a painful time. Being submerged in doing... New beginnings... Marriage and first year of teaching— stretching to seven.

North Dakota State University... Beginning a turning... Models of teaching and process approaches to learning... My start at curriculum... Questioning... Master's degree and a mentor nudging toward further graduate study.

University of Wisconsin and graduate studies: my introduction to critical social theory. Home economics at a turning point... The reconceptualization of the field from a critical science perspective: a time of self-examination, curriculum change—opportunity facing resistance.

The Pennsylvania State University and a Ph.D. program—another special mentor... Still searching for being and a person dimension to inquiry. Hermeneutics and phenomenology discovered, and a centering for my dissertation inquiry. More curriculum projects and more turning—bringing together knowing and being.

The University of Maryland—a place to be what I had been becoming. A group to share my inquiry interests—teaching opportunity for curriculum change and research opportunity with my call to student teachers—a returning to my own turning begun in student teaching.

To know as we are known—the past in our present— to be as we become—questioning schooling—to celebrate as we are celebrated... *These are some of the themes significant for me in my teaching and in my personal and professional journey. They are existential themes that open to the human condition. My knowing has been revealed in my power to* be.

Finding Our Own Voices: Reflections
of a Participant

*Since I was one who helped give shape and direction to our
interpretive inquiry process this first year we came together
as a group, this paper is an attempt to capture the meanings
that grew out of the experience of our group and our place
of speaking as researchers. Many struggles in the form of tensions were revealed in the process of finding ourselves and
our place of speaking in this way of knowing. My struggle
had to do with how much leadership to offer so as not to be
concealing as "expert" but rather revealing as a hermeneutic
traveler on the journey. I also faced the resistance of the
group to reading the philosophers I had come to "revel in"
and the language which for me was a "freeing" experience,
but for the group was an alienating one. Through this struggle, the group gave me the opportunity to really own this
new language in my experience of it, rather than to merely
philosophize about it.*

As a group of seven women coming together throughout the year, we
sought to explore what interpretive inquiry is about or is like by sharing our experiences together as a group as we were engaged in the
process of that exploration. My responsibility now for us, and for others
who would seek this form of inquiry, is to conceptually frame the inquiry as we experienced it in reference to features that are ascribed to
the interpretive orientation. The intent of this framing is not for the
purpose of laying down a method, as that would be contradictory to
the life of the inquiry we sought to understand; we sought to uncover
possibilities for understanding rather than prescriptions. *The design of
such inquiry is said to be retrospective rather than prospective* (Darroch and Silvers 1982), and as such seeks to be accountable to others
by showing what was at play throughout the inquiry (the biography of
the inquiry and group) which led to the interpretations made.

In seeking to recover my own existential commitment in our interpretive inquiry together (responsibility for my own voice, in our

shared dialog both written and verbal), I will attempt to recover the phenomena that seem to have sprung from, or have been uncovered, in the process of our seeking to understand what interpretive inquiry means. I speak from my own biographical standpoint, not *for* the group, but in such a way that may reveal how I have come to interpret what we have revealed together, in display of the process of interpretive inquiry. The value of this kind of inquiry is not assured by "methodological orthodoxy" but rather by the ability of persons to "express a shared experience in an understandable way" (Barritt et al. 1983, 141). That is the intent of this paper and our symposium today. The text we created through our writing and dialog transcriptions is a record of our search for meaning as we came together from diverse backgrounds with different agendas that unfolded throughout our inquiry. From these different perspectives we were able to come to a variety of insights and fuller understanding. What then was the nature of our experience encountering each other through interpretive inquiry?

A Retrospective View of Our Beginnings: What Is Research?

As we first came together as a group, our course was not necessarily charted in the direction of interpretive inquiry, although several of us had our orientation turned in this direction already. With the exception of one of our participants, we for the most part shared a frustration and a "falling out" with the empirical paradigm in our individual research endeavors, which revealed itself in heightened dissonance experienced after several sessions. Our reflection on the meaning of research in our lives revealed some painful encounters.

The stark display of our initial inquiry together catches glimpses of our flirting with casting aside research in the way we have come to understand it, for want of a better way to communicate our "selves" in the significance of what we do. Jana describes the dilemma so vividly in her struggle with wanting to reclaim a prior life of novelist and writer that she left in pursuit of "objective truth," where she now finds that she cannot *be* or speak freely. But what stands behind the words she expresses and the meaning of research that brings out this struggle which reveals itself in such anger? As I hear Jana's words, "maybe this group will help me get out of research, if I can't make my peace with it," I am saddened to think of the debilitating hold one view of research has on persons where the only option appears to be to leave if there cannot be a reconciliation of the different worlds in the research process. On the one hand, Jana seeks a disclosure of self in the research process with a full awakeness of how her "being" in her relationship with teachers is the kind of genuine relationship she would seek to have the teachers share with their students. But then on the other hand, she reveals a skepticism about not wanting to call it research, which in effect communicates the contamination of so precious an encounter of what is real by calling it research. This reveals the question about the place of the researcher and persons studied. *Interpretive inquiry seeks to establish a communicative relationship with persons encountered, and is not seen as a form of inquiry separate from ourselves.* We may cognitively accept that notion, as well as experience it in our way of existing, but then why are we so haunted by "the other" in the way of defining research? As Jana shares: "I can *define* research *exactly* the way I want to, and I can *do* it and I can *be* it and I can *write* it, but other people in my life come in and they have their definition and it *isn't* mine, and they're not going to listen, and they're not interested in listening. Now to some degree I live with that reality too." We began, then, to examine research through different lenses, through our experiences in this group.

"What Has Been the Nature of My Experience in Coming to This Group?"

Although interpretive inquiry is not a technique to be laid down, there are some indirect methods which may be used to help draw out the hidden structures of experience, which we turned to early in our group. *Written descriptions* of our experience in coming to this group served as a way of access for us to *disclose the foundations of our reflections* on research and the group, and it began to be a way for us to experience interpretive inquiry through doing it, and not just talking about it. As Jana said: "I need more experience using the process . . . I can use the language that is there but the process is a little more deep than that. That's where I need help, because that's exactly what I think I'm not doing when I do deal with writing tasks is get beneath the surface of that particular subject." This concern about not being able to get beneath the surface is exactly the driving force of what interpretive inquiry seeks to do: *"to the things themselves,"* the meaning of which is to work out the fore structures of our understandings in terms of the experienced context. *The primacy of experience* is a major element of this inquiry, which is reflected in its "lived context." This calls for us to put aside our preconceived notions about even the most ordinary concepts and events in order to see them in a new way—to ask questions and provide "lived accounts" which may at first appear even simple. But if we are to see what stands behind the words, we must move to the *concrete experience*. And so our search for the meaning of "Lived Experience" began (a new expression that we needed to ground) as we confronted our individual landscapes in our formation as researchers and teachers. The promise was compelling: "Experience is ready to give up its secrets when directly confronted" (Schrag 1969, 87). What were some of our "secrets" revealed then? Our experiences confronted revealed our presences in the act of inquiry—a basic condition for knowledge and understanding in the human sciences and education. *We were finding our places of speaking—and responsibility for our own voices,* our existential commitment (Darroch and Silvers 1982). Within this recovery of our "places and voices," the following foundations or themes emerged from our written descriptions and dialog (reflecting the movement of our inquiry—a "showing" of what was revealed to us).

Expanding Horizons: Anticipation of the Journey

As Diane described it: "Why did I come? That is the easy question. Research! For me, the word is provocative; the process is exhilarating." Similar expressions revealed the anticipation experienced by the group as a whole:

> Sense of wonder—excitement about new journey together
> Chance for dialog encounter
> Recognition of potential for growth from group
> Sought growth-centered haven of colleagues
> Anticipation of intellectual challenge
> Extend knowledge
> Came to learn
> Enjoyment of research
> Opportunity to share research interests
> Seeking more active life of the mind in research and writing

We were ready to face and confront the boundaries of our thinking in the exploration of different forms of inquiry, and we all embraced a receptivity to an expansion of our horizons:

> Understanding a form of inquiry different from one's own is not dependent on an acceptance of its principles or a moral embrace of its meaning. Rather it is a "hearing" of another investigative practice which, as a recognition of difference, brings into view the limits of one's own universals that prereflectively have been taken for granted. (Darroch and Silvers 1982, 233)

Sharing an Orientation of Similar Direction

As a new assistant professor, fresh with degree in hand and the ink barely dry on the dissertation, finding a group of colleagues at a new university who shared a similar concern about the embeddedness of research in the empirical paradigm was like "coming home" for me; I came with a desire to probe further into the philosophy and methodology of interpretive inquiry. Others shared a similar "turning" as expressed in the following:

> Interpretive inquiry is attractive to me in my dissertation
> Came to group out of an invitation and existentialist interest in interpretation
> A "coming home" to kindred souls

As we reflected on "coming" to the group, another element that seemed to have a strong "staying" basis for the group surfaced in reference to the disenchantment with the dehumanization of institutionalized relationships.

Haven from a "Crisis in Humanity": Establishing I-Thou Relationships

As Jana begins, "I have been struggling with the dissonance between work-self and personal-self... all my life my personal-self loses, or has until recently." Others revealed similar calls to being and staying in the group:

> Collegiality at new university
> Fills gap created by institutional competition
> Help in maintaining sanity in a world interested in objective knowledge
> Exciting promise of group to eliminate isolation in a department not sharing interpretive orientation
> Tired of defending interpretive perspective with encrusted empiricists
> Angered to think of person excluded from reward process because of choosing thread of a different texture

Although the group was a place that nurtured an I-Thou way of relating, it began to be the source of dissonance for some, as we addressed the question, "What has this experience meant in my work life?"

> If I address the question honestly, I must say that our encounters cause me to be more frustrated than I ordinarily am. In this group

I have such an opportunity. In real life I am in so many situations where I realize freedom of teachers and students as being seriously circumscribed. I dislike being in such situations, particularly when I feel like the boy with his finger in the dike... This group reinforces my own need to become only what I can become; the outside world tries to cast me in a mold. The lack of fit between my preferred setting and the settings in which I ordinarily find myself becomes a source of frustration. (Louise)

Jessie, in response to a work situation wherein a staff member interrupted a conference she was having with a doctoral student because she wanted to say good-bye, revealed these thoughts:

I thought about this incident many times... Why was she leaving?... I later learned her contract had not been renewed... Into the vacuum created by my empty feelings, justified or not, rushed my concerns about the responsibilities we have towards each other... as a participant in the decision-making process. Which gifts are appropriate at these times? (Jessie)

Jana described Jessie's realization as having to do with the theme of "suddenly *not* being in a group where everyone knows you and understands you, but being a dehumanized member of a dehumanizing institution."

The struggle that was being expressed was related to Heidegger's notion of "Forfeiture": The struggle against giving over to the "They" (wanting to be yourself—wanting to "be," and feeling the pressure of giving over to how others would like you to be). Embedded in the struggle was the striving for freedom and authenticity within the constraints of a technocratic paradigm:

I sometimes feel like I'm trapped in a box. I want to scream out what I know, but feel the scream being stifled in my throat as it seems to fall on deaf ears. They (planning committee) want to break away from a technical image, but cannot see the contradictions in what competency-based ideology is doing. (Francine)

Other struggles were expressed around the tenure process, giving up the I-ness for tenure, the problem of having work respected for its unique contributions and yet questioning whether you sell your soul in the process. As the group became a place of allowing us to "really be" (a haven at first), it was not taken to be an escape or shelter from the world, as the question was continuously posed: "How do I incorporate my being, the aliveness I feel with other persons during encounter, with the outside world?" (Jessie). Jana shared one such encounter:

I am sitting at a kindergarten table, on a tiny chair in a classroom, now calm after a day of active movement. Quiet is inappropriate;

the two teachers and I are talking now, introducing noise into a deaf world (even though one teacher is deaf, we all rely on signed-voiced English). I am much happier here than writing about features and variables. As we look at the deaf children's journals and what they have communicated, Susan, who is deaf, grows more and more excited. She looks like someone seeing validation of her own intuitions and personal knowledge for the first time. I am energized by this encounter; I am not just working in the context where dialog journals occur, but Susan, Jean, and I are also in a unique encounter right now, a dialog where new meaning is being constructed. I want to yell out "This is it!" But there is no one else to see, and no way to record this moment. But I carry it around with me, a week later, just as I carry, embody, the many other epiphanies in my life that come through such I-thou dialogs with others.

Fear of Being

As much as we were expressing the hopes of what this group would contribute to our "being," there was a hesitancy at first about self-disclosure—an almost fleeing in the face of being, as we came to know and trust one another. "I find myself caught by, humming to the word *being,* not a word I like—too soft, and mushy, but there it is—incarnate, personness, just *being,* reflecting faith and trust rather than good works" (Jana). Similar reservations about self were revealed by the group:

> I feel honored to be part of the group where the level of scholarship is far above my own
> How does the group perceive me?
> Initial feeling of reserve in group
> Hesitant about revealing self
> Feel that I am not yet a member of the group
> I am on the periphery
> I am frightened
> Need to "catch up" with group
> Need time to sort out and think
> My silence is my defense

I was experiencing another kind of reservation.

Struggle Between Leadership (Revealing) and Control (Concealing)

As the first meeting unfolded, I sensed some reserve in myself as with the group as a whole. We were a group coming together in dialog, but before we could come together in the "we-ness" of true dialog, we had some barriers to remove in getting to know one another. Although we were united in respect to seeking a support group, it was apparent we had some different journeys in mind and different notions about how to get there ... As I thought about my excited interest in pursuing interpretive inquiry, I found myself holding this enthusiasm somewhat in check as I sensed that maybe I was being too selfish and controlling of the group's direction ... I had a gnawing feeling of exerting too much control. My struggle was at this time how much should I offer in the way of focus and substance? Was more being expected of me? Was I withholding too much? Why was I experiencing this struggle? (I was sensitive to not wanting to be looked at as "expert" wherein that could be concealing. The challenge was to lead in ways that would help in our revealing.) (Francine)

As we were first coming to know one another, we were concerned about initial appearances, which began to give way to trust as we established a communicative relationship through our encounters. This movement seems to be the essence of what Heidegger (1962) had in mind: Relation with others is not one of perception, but of care.

Restorative-Nurturing-Caring: The Pedagogic Relation

Trusting. Restorative. Nurturing. Next session I might even giggle. Perhaps for you, the group, an appropriate heading would be "Inquiry as Being." Right now, for me, an appropriate heading would be "Inquiry as Becoming." I am becoming more trusting, I feel somewhat rejuvenated, and by opening up so completely I've allowed you to nurture. Now I must become more knowledgeable. (Diane)

Mary reveals a similar feeling about the group: "The group has been partly a way of learning to trust yourself."

The expression of care revealed for one another in our group encounters is the essence of the pedagogical relationship, a being (a guiding, a leading) that is oriented toward actualization (van Manen 1984). Caring, as presupposed in these encounters, was experienced in the group in the following ways:

Group nurtures my new being
A feeling of being well-taken-care-of
Helping nature of group in guiding each other through questions
Feeling of fondness and warmth toward each group member
Excited by sense of caring
Came to be with persons I respect and love
Jessie and Louise, a drawing to come—forever their students

A carry-over of this way of being with others was expressed by Mary in reference to her students (the persons in her dissertation inquiry): "I feel confident that by being careful, full of care as Heidegger has it, they and I can be working toward understanding, toward a unity of truth and being." Another element of this "pedagogic way of being" occurs not just in the verbal transmission, but communication that occurs through gestures and expressive looks as well. That element seemed to be significant for some by the very nature of our group composition: all women.

Women Giggling Together without Embarrassment

It seemed important for some in coming to the group that we were all women:

> Importance of being with *women*
> Joined group to work with academic women
> Can giggle together without embarrassment
> Social interest as well

In the life of dialog that calls for a kind of intimacy and sharing through self-disclosure, is it possible for men and women to share horizons as women can with other women or men can with other men? For this group, the dropping of masks where we could "giggle together without embarrassment" seemed to call for a shared understanding only thought possible between women. Maybe it is captured in Jana's reflection: "We can see ourselves, our historical/social selves reflected back from each other." That very perception is one that was reflected, however, by Jane to be somewhat intimidating: "In what ways am I fearful that they (women) will 'see' things and know things that men don't notice?" Despite her acknowledgment of fondness and warmth towards *each* individual in the group, she questions why so many of her animosities are directed towards women in the field. Her reflections found their expression in the following struggle.

Living the Struggle: Annoyance and Commitment

Jane reveals in her reflections on coming to the group that her preparations for the Interpretive Inquiry Group followed a consistent pattern each month:

> Annoyance (I don't have time ... I should be writing)
> I'll just go and won't say anything (I don't understand phenomenology)
> Obsessed with logistics of getting there (what to wear—directions)
> Uncomfortable reestablishing relationships with women, a few I don't know very well (I'm more comfortable around men)
> I grow enthusiastic as each evening goes on

Jana reveals a similar struggle: "Each month I wear down until three days before the meeting I start saying, 'I won't go; I am too busy; all we do is talk and nothing changes'... Somehow I find myself on the road at 7:00, driving madly for thirty minutes across the city and country-side to reach the meeting place." When asked by an outsider what the group was like, she responded: "It's like stopping by somebody's office and having a chat—because it's where you get your good ideas." The commitment was there, as expressed by a group recognition: "We may not remember our assignment, but we always come!" Maybe our call came from living out our struggles and tensions there in the group together. I was acutely aware of this need for living out our individual struggles in finding ourselves first before going on to gain further un-derstanding of this inquiry, but I was experiencing a pull in another direction, a different struggle.

Floating and Idle Talk

At the second session as we shared articles that reflected our concerns about curriculum and teacher education, I began to feel that my inter-est again was different:

> I felt somewhat of a struggle within myself to want to engage in common reading wherein we could surface the interpretation to-gether—Merleau Ponty and Heidegger were pronounced in my in-terests. I began to be fearful that we might get too preoccupied with idle talk, that is, a surface or groundless floating where we have difficulty making the dialog our own. I began to hear an inner voice telling me I should help provide a focus or a grounding... I sought to look at my own lived experience of interpretive inquiry, and sought to enter it more fully, but I felt like I was floating—I couldn't seem to find an anchor or common footing to approach our inquiry together. (Francine)

This was my personal struggle. Jana recognized it too in her comment: "I think when we get into continuously revolving discussions, it's usu-ally because we haven't been able to ground it in anything." Another struggle was present for Jana as well.

A "Coming Out" and a "Returning Home": Shedding the Conceptual Skill of the Empirical Paradigm

Jana, who described herself as the angry one in the group, found her-self working through an inner struggle (coming out from the empirical paradigm in educational psychology and returning to being a writer of personal interpretation). The anger seemed to arise from "living in si-lence for so long... not speaking, living behind a mask, hoping to be accepted and acknowledged by those in power." This struggle was revealed in her written description in the following forms:

> Frustration with dominant paradigm which doesn't allow me to be
> Sees educational research as a sham
> Midlife crisis of reexamination
> This is a "coming out" (from behind questionnaires)
> Fear about moving from potential for impact to having none
> Contradiction experienced: Wanting to be accepted by those in power (research community) and now can't stand to live in that paradigm
> Questions: Who matters?
> Feeling that group has allowed me to "get out" of research
> Also seems like a "return" to that of being a writer (personal interpretation)
> Caught by the word *being*

Jana describes herself as "being in a transition—shedding an old skin and feeling vulnerable." A similar paradigm struggle was revealed, in a broader context, to the world outside where research is done: the schools.

Lived Culture vs. Commodity Culture: Feeling the Tension

Louise addressed this tension:

> I seem to dwell in two worlds relative to my research endeavors. My interests—stemming back to my days as a literature major— are in the quality of the "lived experience." However, since I work with students who frequently are planners and policy makers, I am perpetually struggling with questions relative to dealing with the masses, but in an existential level. Is such possible? How does a state make requirements for schooling based on the lived worlds of learners?

The question of using the interpretive process to gain access to lived experience with teachers in classrooms was pursued in the following exchange.

Louise: When you're dealing with the practical knowledge of teachers you do some of this.

Mary: The skills test and stuff like that, you know, it has nothing to do with what's going on. You give the children a piece of paper to do for an hour a day, and you know it has nothing to do with what's going on in the life of the classroom.

Jana: ... But they (the testing people) are being hard scientists who want only hard data; they're able to be removed from the event, and ask teachers to send them test scores, and reports, or whatever.

The question, then, arose of the problems of individual versus culture and its historical context within interpretive inquiry:

Jane: Can one person hold all the culture? How do we get from one individual biography to the larger group context? How will this help me to get to teachers' culture?

Fran: The individual has a historical context. Knowledge is socially constructed. In phenomenology the intent is not just to describe, but also to transcend ... One cannot do interpretive work without movement toward change.

Jane: I think it's arrogant if we think that when we understand how a group operates then you can change. Culture isn't open to deliberate one-person onslaught of change.

Fran: Change for the sake of improving the human condition. We don't impose change but provide the conditions for others to seek change, an empowering.

Mary: Freire is talking about hopeless conditions for people.

Fran: The conditions were different, but idea the same—to break into false consciousness ... and help people (teachers) realize their options ... break into power structures.

Jana: Only because of groups like this can we go back and live dangerously. You are not dangerous by yourself. Only in a group can you get the language. I couldn't do this without this dialog. Out there there is no shared reality. We owe a debt of gratitude to the empiricists for our being here!

What Jana is saying here is similar to a Freirian notion of change and is also reflected in Darroch and Silvers (1982): Finding out what an experience is like in the words of the one experiencing it creates a new discourse that is empowering. It gives power back to individuals and does not merely hold onto an expert's view as educator or researcher or philosopher. We were beginning to "own" our way of talking about interpretive inquiry, by experiencing it, but not without a struggle.

The Uninitiated: Language and the House of Being or Not Being?

I came to this group enamored with my prior experience of doing interpretive inquiry, hoping to grapple with the "great works" of those writing about interpretive philosophy so as to "ground" my understanding in the tradition which I had come to value and practice. I came with a language that I had newly acquired from my hermeneutic phenomenological study, and which I felt to be revealing of a different way of thinking that I was thrilled about having found. I thought everyone would experience the same exhilaration about a language that helped break the empirical spell heretofore cast on research. As I read one of the reviews of our proposal for AERA, suggesting that we see beyond the language "dripping with a heavy dose of newly discovered educational jargon," I was painfully reminded of the alienation that language can create.

Language was a concern that surfaced again and again in our writing and in our discourse. After an attempt at some "grounding" by reading Darroch and Silvers, Jane reveals her frustration: "Is this process one for the elite? Is it a new set of jargon or metalanguage?" She talked about her own research with teachers and their discourse in stories to give language to what they're doing. The goal for her is to deal in simple, clear language—not elitist jargon. And Mary said: "I don't like the language, but like the process of looking." Other concerns reflected in the first written description were:

> Overwhelmed by vocabulary
> Are you asking me to exchange one language for another?
> Always comes back to language—where being is connected to saying it

Or as Jessie questions: "Is it necessary, important to invent new words, to propose new definitions for commonly used words, or words that the 'others' use? Is seemingly cumbersome language necessary to celebrate one's uniqueness or to communicate the notion that there are viable alternatives to more common research methods?" Another concern was expressed about work with school people, trying to communicate in a language where there is shared understanding—a translation being necessary. Such a concern might be "grounded" in Gadamer's view of language and the hermeneutical problem:

> Every translation is at the same time an interpretation ... If we really master a language, then no translation is necessary ... For you understand a language by living it ... Thus the hermeneutical problem is not one of the correct mastery of language, but of the proper understanding of that which takes place through the medium of language. (Gadamer 1975, 346)

Our hermeneutical problem became clear as we sought to understand what was taking place in our inquiry through language.

Hermeneutical Borderline

Gadamer sheds light here again:

> Translation, like all interpretation, is a highlighting. A translator must understand that highlighting is part of his task. Obviously he must not leave open whatever is not clear to him, but must declare himself. Yet there are border-line cases in which ... something is, in fact, unclear. But precisely these hermeneutical border-line cases show the straits in which the translator finds himself ... He must state clearly how he understands. (p. 348)

I find a clear example of this occurring in our September meeting, as portions of the dialog reveal. Jana was talking about a change in her research focus, wherein she wants to study the event, "not analyze and manipulate its residue." The dialog unfolded in the following manner.

Jane: I just have one difference, umm, you said the word *residue?* ... Well one of the things I was reacting to, umm ... let me turn to Diane's writing here first. She says governs—hermeneutics governs the search for meaning and temporality seems to be a salient feature. It is an act of historical understanding. Understanding is the key ... This snapped it into a whole construct for me. I have, like I teach social studies methods, and the first day every year, I always say, and I have to go to language for this, is that I'm trying to explain what social studies is, you know, and I say, everything, even the things that are happening right now have happened in the past. I mean, as soon as something happens, then, it's an event that happened in the past. And the only way you get to it ... is by examining the *residue* of social events. So I really like the idea of residue because I look to symbols; it is, and language really is residue. I mean, as soon as the event has happened, all you have is human testimony, whether it's an old artifact that's been there for two thousand years or whether it's just what you've said about what I have written. So, I think there's the issue of whether you want to manipulate it or not, but it's all examination of residue. So I like the word.

Jana: I think when I was writing it, it was more the idea of having little bits and pieces somehow separated out from your past.

Jane: But you get residue.

Jana: The writing we do here I like. Writing about this I do not
            consider somehow analyzing or manipulating the event
            or its meanings ... It is historical understanding ... If one
            looks on residue as real, as pieces of persons left behind
            and events that one encounters, then all we're doing here
            is part of trying to capture this inquiry as it goes along,
            and I think we are going to value our pieces of writing ...
            There's a different attitude toward this group and its data.

Jane: I still am having trouble with the word *manipulate* ... I
            want to go back to the difference in understanding and
            explaining; cause I think that's where it's at; I don't think
            it's manipulation. I mean, the thing that I'm trying to get
            at is just how do you understand and explain ... Don't we
            sort of explain things to understand them, so I'm not real
            sure if it's a dichotomy ... You know, I think it's almost an
            approach to life ... What's so fascinating, in one of our
            introductory courses when you teach about writing ob-
            jectives, the first word they're taught not ever to use is
            understand!

Jane: It seems to me much of the essence of what the interpre-
            tive inquiry process is, such as we're doing is effecting
            some changes, some *re*examination. I don't find that char-
            acteristic of the traditional research model that we get
            into, where it *claims* to examine assumptions, the facts,
            the truth, but in effect only tries to *prove* that which is
            assumed.

At this point we were beginning to reveal our differences in understanding and clearly trying to articulate what was unclear, which led to
the questioning of assumptions.

A Crisis of Question: Unveiling Assumptions

A most powerful confrontation of self, regarding assumptions about
persons, strikes at the core of understanding found in existence:

> You see, I guess I find that I'm in a position more frequently here
> defending the other, and it, the true dissonance is not created out-
> side, and when I first wrote restorative nurturance, I was quot-
> ing Jana, and it was what you said at the meeting I last attended.
> When I heard those words I was in shock! And it was like, oh my
> heavens—opposite from you! And, and I was traumatized that I
> was so apart, and that's why I spoke of it. I was not sharing that
> sense with the group, and I had to look closely with them, having

written the dissertation and having worked so closely with them, having written, umm, after literally, Jessie giving me Madsen's book, *The Image of Man,* and talking about persons as proactive, and all the words I wrote about, and then turned around and set them down to multiple regression, and talked about accounting for variance, and the struggle *I'm* having is trying to determine if the assumptions *are* different. And Francine, I was *so* pleased, when I read your pages, and at the end, we had asked the same question. Can a person, umm, hold both threads at the same time and still try to weave a pattern that makes sense, and, that's why language is so important, and it's so important in the research that *you* do, and it's so *distant* from me! And that's why when we were talking, and Jane said when we force people into a forced-choice question-naire, we try to quantify that, have we taken away the subjective meaning of the experience and I said, or have we substituted a common language so that we can speak with persons about them-selves. I'm not sure, and this is my struggle, to see whether I'm giving lip service to my assumptions about persons and it's fright-ening as hell. (Diane)

And then Diane said: "Thank you for forcing me to speak." Does this not then express the heart of what our inquiry attempted and realized, what we also find in Darroch and Silvers:

> Introducing a form of inquiry in this sense allows not only a first entrance for others but a first leaving for oneself. It is, for those who undertake to recover their own movement-in-inquiry, an at-tempt through difference and doubt to confront and disclose a si-lence—a silence which announces itself when we have arrived at the limits of shared understanding. (1982, 233)

References

Barritt, L., T. Beekman, H. Bleeker, and K. Mulderij (1983). The world through children's eyes: Hide and seek & peekaboo. *Phenomenol-ogy + Pedagogy, 1* (2), 140–161.

Darroch, V. and R. V. Silvers (1982). *Interpretive human studies: An introduction to phenomenological research.* Washington, DC: Uni-versity Press of America.

Gadamer, H-G. (1975). *Truth and method.* New York: Crossroad.

Heidegger, M. (1962). *Being and time.* New York: Harper & Row.

Schrag, C. O. (1969). *Experience and being.* Evanston, IL: Northwestern University Press.

van Manen, M. (1984). Reflections on teacher experience and pedagogic competence. In E. Short (ed.), *Competence: Inquiries into its meaning and acquisition in educational settings.* Washington, DC: University Press of America, 141–158.

My Journey from Knowing to Being in Phenomenology: Caught in the Language and Pursuit of Method

I began the journey this year wanting to know how I could "enter the question" as I nudged the group in the direction of trying to understand the meaning of Gadamer's Hermeneutic Priority of the Question. As we told our individual stories of the central struggles in our lives as educators and what questions these stories were answers to, I began to see my concern about a method for questioning in a different light. As our work proceeded to uncover central metaphors giving expression to our way of being as educators, I was painfully reminded how I was trying to throw off metaphors that to me were reminders of a technical orientation my profession had been labeled with, which for others were natural expressions of their way of being. This led me to question what it is like to live in a metaphor of one's own choosing as opposed to somebody else's imposition. I also chose to exercise my interest in interpreting the central ideas of the questions that each of our texts were an answer to, which all seemed to be responses to a central question of "What is it like to be in teaching together?" The group became a memory store of lived metaphors bringing new meaning to curriculum and teaching.

From the vantage point of being one of the travelers in a journey that was begun with colleagues three years ago to understand interpretive inquiry, pausing to reflect on how the journey was experienced differently at the beginning from what the experience has offered up to us now seems like a way to capture how the course of the journey has changed us. As we entered the journey and some persons described themselves as the "angry one," "the perennial student," or "the one without a question," I could have been described as the one "dripping with a heavy dose of newly discovered language"—*jargon* as some might have called it! I wanted to "revel" in that newly discovered language of phenomenology, which others in the group have since pointed to with great affectation as they described their own state as being "in quicksand" or "in a quagmire" with the language! So we certainly entered the journey at different starting points, but we were drawn together, or united, as we "came to the group" in order to find our own places of speaking—to find a better way of communicating our *selves* in the significance of what we do as teachers and researchers. Experiencing this new form of inquiry was, then, a first entrance for some—but for me I think it allowed a "first leaving." I was attempting to recover my *own* movement-in-this-inquiry—to *own it as mine,* rather than to live in someone else's language. In that sense, then, I have seen my participation in the journey as a sense of struggle, in which the group allowed the right amount of tension—pulling me *from* the reliance on this new language to express myself to the opportunity to *be* what the language was creating for me. I wanted to continue to *read* the works of those who were giving rise to my new speaking—and they wanted rather to *talk*—to voice and hear one another in the nurturing of I-Thou relationships. We did not really raise too many questions in the beginning, and if we did they were more in the form of "Does this sound right?" or "Is this what you meant?"—our personal fears and inadequacies in this new terrain and group were apparent. We *voiced* those initial experiences at AERA three years ago. As we were reflecting then on why we "came to the group," we are now giving pause to reflect on the "staying power" of the group—what is it that gives us reason to remain in our group?

We initially came to the group as we chose to form our own context for conversation because our institutions did not allow the kinds of conversations we sought to have. I would like to suggest that it has been the power of our *questioning* that has kept us together in such an extraordinary way—but that might have been my struggle to help others see this year! At least that is what we sought to do at the beginning of this year—to look at the questions that our individual texts as well as our group text were an answer to. The centrality of our questions, however, did not come freely—in fact, they were probably resisted due to the way in which we were all seeking to throw off prior ways of perceiving questioning—as challenging or interrogating persons—rather than as a way to help make our texts speak.

My Story as Journey: How Do I Enter the Question and "Be" in My New Language?

I entered the journey with our group this year wanting to know "How do I Enter the Question?" This particular question was central for me as I was asking myself, "How do I help students gain insight into their experience of student teaching by asking questions which open the way to understanding?" We began by each telling stories about what the central themes were in our lives as educators. We chose stories to help understand who we are and to consider them as ways we have chosen to give meaning to our lives. As suggested by Novak, "To tell a story with one's life is simply to act" (1971, 41). The story is a narrative, then, that links sequences in our lives over time. The story I began with needs to be retold here for me to make the central connection to what my experience with the group this year has been like.

I began my story by sharing that the central quest for me in my life as an educator at the moment has to do with the struggle of throwing off the technocratic in teacher education and restoring a sense of the human venture in teaching. As I am living in that struggle daily with my student teachers once again this semester, I am feeling the need to confront *what stands behind that struggle for me? What in my experience has brought me to this point?* I search for language that will help bring my experience into a greater conscious awareness so as to reveal the themes that are central to me. The metaphor of journey pushes most strongly here again—as a point of access. I might liken some of the elements of a journey to the struggle in which I am finding myself. There is a starting point and generally an ending point—and the terrain in between is an unknown. There are different expectation states one has as the journey is begun. Sometimes the journey is very directed and orderly, and at other times it is much more open to what is encountered along the way.

I began the telling of my journey at a point when I was first introduced to a new language in my graduate education that gave me new ways of thinking about education in general, and my teaching practice in particular. Phenomenology was the new departure point, but before this new departure into the new terrain, the background for what I brought to the journey is significant. Up until this point, teaching for me was the perfecting of technique and a search for writing the perfect objective that always seemed so elusive. That directive journey was begun for me in my student teaching experience, wherein the end of that short journey was less than fulfilling—it was debilitating! I felt I had not mastered these techniques, and questioned if I was really "cut out" to be a teacher? (What does that metaphor imply?) I spent seven years trying to answer that question—teaching home economics in the public schools. Techniques seemed relatively easy to master within a subject area that seemed to pride itself in the preparation of products. I never seemed to raise questions of teaching practice that went beyond technique. So when I found myself face to face with the language I encountered in phenomenology as I began graduate work, I felt a whole new world was opening up. At first I was taken with the terminology and new ideas and the philosophers who gave me that language to revel in: specifically Heidegger and his image of the "Shepherd of Being." I sought to be that kind of shepherd with my student teachers for whom I was responsible. I pursued my phenomenological journey, then, with great enthusiasm—open to what I might discover as I tried my new wings, as I was taken with Spiegelberg's advice: "Better some early dilettantism than mature sterility!" (1975, 2).

Where am I now in this journey with, in, and through phenomenology? I am five years beyond the first real journey I took (in my dissertation project) and have since encountered four groups of student teachers—wherein I have approached my work with them through a phenomenological perspective. I find that the language comes easily for me now, as I go to great lengths to describe the journey I seek to map out with great flourish in my syllabus. My beginning and end of the journey is explicit in the following idea expressed by Krishnamurti: To understand life is to understand ourselves and that is both the beginning and end of education (1964). The valued end, or possibly even the process of reaching that kind of understanding, is revealed in my statement on page 1 of the course syllabus about the focus on the lived world of teaching, wherein I suggest that "the quality of the experience in this course can be enhanced when you, as student teachers, personally and autonomously come to understand your own life worlds and how these are connected to taking action in the everyday life world of teaching . . . Inquiry into the meaning of one's existence (ways of being) is essential to the concept of experience just as much as are ways of knowing." I also suggest that "the intent of this course is not a focus on a 'how to' approach in the sense of learning techniques, but rather it is designed to be an experience in making connections between the surface components of what you plan for and actually do in teaching with the meaning this has for human development and understanding" (syllabus, p. 1). What I am realizing the more I try to orchestrate this kind of encounter is the *supreme irony* of my present search: I am once again in the pursuit of a method, if you will (heaven forbid I dare not call it technique!) of ways in which to ask the kinds of questions which will reach beyond or behind their words they use to describe their experiences—and mine for that matter! I have turned to Gadamer (1975) in that search for the essence of the question, which is to have sense—direction—and open up, as it were, the being of the object of our search—to preserve an openness to that which we seek to understand. But then I am reminded by Gadamer that there is no such thing as a method of learning to ask questions—of learning to see what needs to be questioned. Gadamer also suggests that, in order to be able to ask a question, one must want to know, which involves knowing that one does not know. I know that I do not know yet the way in which to ask a question that orients the student teachers, myself, and the subject of our examination to the world. Phenomenology seeks to enter that world through relation—a way of finding ourselves in a relation of being-in-the-world.

Looking at experience through my discipline has been sought through a conceptual way of knowing, rather than entering it through an engagement in *being*. What is at the center of my struggle now is casting off this dependence on a method for doing this (or possibly redefining method) so as to enter dialog in the spirit of my metaphor—a journey that we engage in together, side by side as we encounter each other in the world, and not merely face to face. This is not a dyadic I-Thou way of relating that I seek, but rather it is a triadic one: teacher and student seeking to understand the object of our investigation (teaching) with each other *in the world* (Scudder and Mickunas 1985).

In essence, that has been what the experience has been for me in the group this year. The central theme in this experience then has been a triadic way of relating with each other in the group as we have sought to uncover questions that our texts have given an answer to— and in that pursuit I want to recount the way in which our questioning has allowed certain themes for me to arise in my pursuit of method. Actually the greatest insight has been for me to see method in a different light. My story, then, has been created around my search for a way to questioning—in my own questioning of the questions to see what stands behind them.

Creating New Metaphors and Redefining the Meaning of Method

Early on in our conversation this year, we came to recognize how central metaphor was in the telling of our stories, and this is what I want to begin with as I recount the questions raised of my story and other stories told. We all seemed to recognize how fundamentally metaphorical our conceptual system is in terms of how we both think and act, as Lakhoff and Johnson (1980) suggest. Our language used is the expression of this underlying conceptual system.

As questions were raised about my story—the one Louise and Mary asked unearthed in me a recognition of metaphors I no longer wanted to own! Their question which prompted these stirrings was: The missing link in your story is *What was it that drew you to your phenomenological turning and orientation?* As I thought about that, I knew that I was seeking to create new ways of seeing as I was struggling to throw off the control I felt in my discipline that was so product oriented. And the two strongest associations for me in that product orientation were *foods* and *clothing*. But just as I was seeking to throw off those past conceptual lenses for giving meaning to what I do, Louise was busy surfacing the powerfully "nourishing" metaphor of *Ideas and Food* in her "dishing it up with doctoral students," and Diane was artfully weaving her tapestry of *Quilt Metaphor!* As she talked about not having to rip the seams (ideas) but that they could be resewn, Jessie shared that it varies with the fabric—if you start ripping it destroys some fabric! Diane suggested she wouldn't have returned to our group if she had had to rip out her seams (ideas)! What that exchange generated in me was the fact that I was busy running as fast as I could (probably from too much seem ripping!) from these two associations in my profession, and in the process was denying a central part of my *inheritance* (the metaphor named by Mary). Lakhoff and Johnson say that new metaphors have the power to create a new reality, and in essence, my turn to a new language in phenomenology was indeed that attempt. I was seeking to throw off a conceptual system embedded in a technical orientation, wherein the remnants of that way of thinking and acting were caught up for me in the connection to foods and clothing. For Louise and Diane to choose these metaphors as beautiful illustrations for seeing their world and action in it was acceptable, and although there was humor along with Louise "cooking up a storm," it was not a stigma to her. If they had been my "metaphors of choice," I would have felt them to be a hallmark normally associated with my profession as stereotyped—so I was therefore denying them. It led me to raise some questions as to *What is it that gives rise to one's change of metaphors? What constitutes a change in one's metaphors to comprehend experience and give direction to our lives? What is it like to live in a metaphor of one's own choice as opposed to somebody else's imposition?*

As I reflected further on our conversation that evening I recognized that in my work with student teachers I am really in essence seeking to introduce some new metaphors in order to allow new ways of thinking about the world, as I seek to push off the technocratic mentality. As I was using a language that opened up new worlds for me, talking in terms of *being* and *experiencing* the *journey of teaching,* and making personal connections to the *life world of classrooms,* rather than performance, behavior, and measurement, I was well aware that my students did not own that language. And so my passion for wanting to develop a way of questioning that would allow a new seeing to come forward was heightened. Louise observed how *different* owning that language might be if one encounters it as an undergraduate where I was seeking to introduce it, rather than encountering it as a graduate student as I had. Diane raised some questions at that point which began to point the way for me as to a different meaning of method. She asked: *"What happens when the students take the journey themselves as teachers? Is there someone else with whom they can travel? What about the lone traveler?"* I began to see that my approach of choosing to take a side-by-side journey with them was for me a matter of being with them in the world—a way of relating—one that I hoped would carry over into their future teaching lives. So the notion of my search for a method to do this cannot be externally imposed or artificially created and then learned as a method. It has to be lived. As Mary said, "You're searching *with* them. They *see* the way you are." Seeing the *teacher* in her being was a nice thought for me; my own sense of being is revealed in the process by the way in which I was choosing to *be* with them in teaching. It was pushing strongly at the phenomenological notion for me of teacher and student in a side-by-side relation seeking to understand the object of our inquiry: *teaching.* What I began to realize in my pursuit of method was that I was seeking ways of making a new orientation more accessible. So as the question was raised later as to *What is the meaning of method?* I began to see that it is to be seen in relation to our way of being—*how we live what we think.* It is revealed more in our speaking from our *search to know* rather than from *what* we know; hence it begins to be most strongly revealed through our questioning. I began to relax and live in the tension, then, somewhat, in my pursuit of a method for questioning that would illustrate the kind of questioning I thought I needed to develop. I would continue to ask in our search for knowing together. It was a powerful illustration for me, though, of how the pursuit of method is a strong carry over from the technocratic orientation, and as one's orientation changes, ways to enter that orientation and how you help others enter that orientation require a rethinking. The use of language and the action consistent with that language are the most powerful illuminators.

In addition to the insights gained from the questions raised of my story, the experience of the journey for me this year also has to do with how our questions in the group emerged and that they truly did "open the way" for helping to make our texts speak. The way for me to make best sense of this is to illustrate the unraveling of the questions in our texts as they occurred through out our conversations with brief excerpts of those questions. The answers have been forthcoming in each interpretation given by each member of the group—so my focus is the question.

Teaching is Creating a Context

As Jessie was addressing her three central themes in teaching (relationship, collaboration, and context) questions arose like the following:

How did your role change in the experience of team teaching?

How is context a way in which you see your themes brought together?

What was your experience with different contexts that brought new insights for you?

These beginning questions reveal our attempt to help her surface what the themes central in her teaching were like for her as she lived them. These were followed by three very penetrating questions of meaning:

What do we recognize about our way of being with another person in teaching that helps us reveal things about ourselves?

How do two people construct a joint metaphor for teaching together?

What is it like to be in teaching together?

(This question surfaced early on in the year and was to become the central question to which all of our stories seemed to be an answer to within our experience of the group.)

Teaching Is Creating the Context for the Authentic Voice of the Teacher

In Jane's work with teachers, her central question seemed to be her concern about what kind of role she plays in bringing out the authentic voice of the teacher? Questions that surfaced here also progressed from some "why" and "how kinds" in the probing of her experience to ones of greater opening:

Why do we want to bring out the authentic voice of the teacher?

When you ask for the authentic voice of teachers, why are you discontent with your own voice? (An interesting question posed of Jane that arose from her initial question).

Other questions surfaced in Jane's work that directly linked to questions of meaning:

What is the context for authentic voices to be heard?

How do we help teacher stories from degenerating into "what worked" kinds of episodes?

What questions were teachers trying to answer?

What question lies behind their behavior?

An interesting exchange about questions began to surface here that pointed to some unsettling thoughts about asking questions, which was a theme that we returned to later:

When I tell a story, do I always have a question?

What prompts a story?

If we don't ask questions, how do we prevent the stories from lying there?

Teaching Is Creating a Context of Comfort Within Anxiety

As Louise approached her central theme of "dishing it up with doctoral students," her interest was in creating a context that would nourish doctoral students so her metaphor of *Ideas as Food* and *Home as Comfort* were especially powerful. Many of her questions in the beginning had to do with ways of creating that kind of environment (a method of sorts):

How does an adviser keep fit for this kind of journey?
How do we develop settings where people feel more passionate about what they do?
How do you get a good mix of ingredients?
In what ways can we be a community of persons working on the dissertation?
What does it mean to have comfort in the process of dishing it up?

A question that seemed to open the way here was:

Maybe you want to think about all aspects of the metaphor of home for you? What is it about that environment that is relational to the kind of environment you are seeking to create in the classroom?

Teaching Science as More Than Inheritance

As Mary questioned the teaching of science from a closed-inheritance sort of way, her interest was in helping students look at what is most intrinsically interesting in their natural world, and it was her belief that students do not need to know all the complicated things of science. Questions that emerged seemed to point to what sort of experience this teaching would be:

How do *you* relate to inheritance?
Is it important to see connections?
What is basic to know? Is it knowledge to function in our lived world or to function in a scientific world?
How do we prepare people to teach these subjects?
Aren't you really asking the question of how you help teachers enter into a relationship with the object of what they seek to help students understand?
Do we enter into a relationship or deal with an inheritance?

Teaching Is Choosing Wicked Problems and Caring

Diane was struggling with how she goes about choosing a question in her attempt to help students focus on "wicked problems"—those that have tenable solutions—rather than "puzzle problems"—those which have final solutions. In posing a central question for herself she was asking:

In real life problems can you be objective?
(Her response was no—subjectivity is always involved)

Other questions were:

If I care enough to pursue a question of meaning, what is the nature of the dialectic?
How do I pose the question?
What am I seeking?

Our Questioning of Questioning

As we were reflecting on the dialectic of question and answer that came through in the telling of our stories, the following dialog excerpts are particularly revealing, displaying our sense of struggle:

Jessie: I'm finding it difficult to look from the inside out. I don't know where these questions are coming from. That's my dilemma.

Diane: I had difficulty writing questions—I'm still back at having to write narratives to myself. I wrote my piece for this evening and I don't have a single question!

Mary: My questions are more like: Why did you say that? People seemed to comment more than raise questions. I think that's one of the dynamics of the group. We try to enrich each other's thought rather raise questions to challenge.

Louise: I think about Dillon's (1981) work on questioning.

Francine: You mean you think questions get in the way?

Jana: Challenging questions are more the company of men. There are other ways of generating knowledge than questions.

Francine: But these aren't challenge questions. It's like—the sense making process. It's raising questions of the text to make it speak—not of the person. It's the way the question helps to point to an insight that is not threatening or challenging. That sense relates very well with how women relate. It seems as if it is the dominant way of questioning that we are fighting.

Jessie: I think I ask too many masculine questions—"how do you justify that?" Maybe we need to look at the nature of our questions.

Francine: What is it when we are alone with our texts, raising questions, that is different from the group? Is it more difficult to do with one's own text? Are we afraid of what we are confronting with ourselves?

Jessie: Something is missing there. Moving from We-I. That social aspect is missing. Here I am alone—there is no "other."

Francine: Could we look at the question with "the other"—as our way of relating in the world with something we are seeking to understand? How did questions we raised of one another allow that relating in the world to be expressed? The questions pointed us to look at something—which we were maybe not conscious of as we were sharing it. We saw what connected in us—our meaning making of what we were saying. Is that a way of connecting with oneself that somebody else has helped us uncover?

Jessie: In making those connections I was starting all over again with my own questions.

Francine: That could be a part of it. The questions that we raised allowed us to have some new insights again. That's the focus of the question that I see—how they pointed to something that we ourselves did not see. How do we have continued dialog then with the way in which the questions pointed?

In our struggle to move away from the dominant notion of questions as challenging or seeking predetermined answers, we were finding that they were difficult to generate or even see in what we *had* generated. I believe our questioning did provide our insights and also gave rise to another element of our discourse—*metaphors*. It was after this discussion that Diane shared her beautiful *Quilt Metaphor* with themes like the following:

We found ourselves weaving patterns—different colors and designs, but with similar threads
Connectedness and meaning making
Persons-to-persons together weaving a fabric
Quilt brings warmth, comfort and caring
Stitches were never ripped out
We became teachers posing questions for which there may be no final answers for terminating our inquiry
We've built faith believing in our journey
To persons—to ideas—to questions—to a journey

What Question Has Our Text Been an Answer to?

What surfaced in our pondering of questions and the meaning found through the images created by Diane's metaphor was finally the question that our texts and experience of the journey were an answer to: *What is it like to be in teaching together in this group?* and *How does this relationship that we have established here help us take a look at the kind of relationships that we are fostering in our own classes?* Additional questions that surfaced here this evening were:

How do we live in our metaphors?
As we enter the metaphor, how do we experience it?
How do we get into the metaphor and then experience it once we are there?

Metaphor now seemed to be as central (if not more) than our questioning. This led me to raise the following questions:

What brings us to the metaphors we have chosen to talk about what we do?
What were we asking that allowed that metaphor to come through?

As we came back to reflect on our conversation across disciplines, what began to be clear to us was the fact that it has been the *stance* taken within our disciplines and not the disciplines themselves (as suggested by Louise) that has given rise to our metaphors we use to organize our world. As we sought to develop and claim a new orientation, we began creating new metaphors together. "If there were any walls for me in this journey," said Diane, "It was not knowing the language. I couldn't join the meaning-making until I learned the language." That brings us right back to the notion of what occurs in conversation as suggested by Gadamer (1975): A common language is found which coincides with the very act of understanding. The full realization of conversation comes when something is expressed that is not only mine or the person who speaks—but what is held in common through language.

As we relate this recognition through our experience to curriculum, it might be, as Louise suggests, that we maybe should approach our courses on curriculum more from the perspective of how metaphor guides curriculum. We would come up with some very different approaches that would help change our language if we lived the metaphors together—not only in our language but in our actions as well.

In closing, I would like to suggest another question that I have surfaced from my reflection on the experience with the group: How have each of us in the group become a memory store of that which gives meaning to teaching and curriculum? As an answer to that question for me, I would enter it through a favorite quote of mine by Schubert:

> Live as if your life were a curriculum for others, and balance that principle by realizing that every life you meet could be a curriculum for you if you perceive with sufficient perspective. (1986, 423)

The group's memory store as to how they became a curriculum for me can be framed in each of their central questions and metaphors:

Jessie: *What is it to enter a relation?*
"Teaching is creating a context."
Louise: *What does it mean if we are ministering (dishing it up) with doctoral students?*
"Teaching is creating a context of comfort within anxiety."
Jane: *In what manner do I give rise to the authentic voice of the teacher?*
"Teaching is creating a social context for those who are silent to be able to speak."
Diane: *Which set of assumptions best fits myself as a researcher— a teacher?*
"Teaching is creating a fabric that no one person will own. As we query about what matters, the pattern the cloth will take emerges."
Mary: *How does teaching relate to our everyday experiences?*
"Teaching is moving beyond our inheritance."
Francine: *How do I enter the question?*
"Teaching is the pursuit of questioning in my search to know through my being."

References

Dillon, J. T. (1981). To question or not to question during discussions: II Non-questioning techniques. *Journal of Teacher Education, 32,* 15–20.

Gadamer, H-G. (1975). *Truth and method.* New York: Crossroad.

Krishnamurti, J. (1964). *Think on these things.* New York: Harper & Row.

Lakhoff, G., and M. Johnson (1980). *Metaphors we live by.* Chicago: The University of Chicago Press.

Novak, M. (1971). *Ascent of the mountain, Flight of the dove.* New York: Harper & Row.

Schubert, W. H. (1986). *Curriculum: Perspective, paradigm, and possibility.* New York: Macmillan.

Scudder, J. R., and A. Mickunas (1985). *Meaning, dialogue and enculturation: Phenomenological philosophy of education.* Washington, DC: University Press of America.

Spiegelberg, H. (1975). *Doing phenomenology.* The Hague: Martinus Nijoff.

Destining of Being through Technological Knowing: The Saving Power of Turning and Questioning

This year I truly experienced the hermeneutic priority of the question as I was "caught" by the question Ted raised of me last year at AERA. He pointed me to see new meaning through the grounds of my existence in a profession from which I was busy seeking to disavow. I experienced a turning or a re-turning to reunderstand a technological way of knowing. The turning brought me to a revisiting of my own student teaching experience, which recovered my turning that was surfacing at that time in my transcendence of "doing" to allow a place for "being." These reflections gave new meaning to "making" and helped me restore a sense of caring to a way of knowing that had been technologically determined, which allowed for the possibility of seeing a new relationship to the bondage of my identity I had been fighting.

In an issue of the *Journal of Curriculum Theorizing* (Fall 1987), former graduate students and colleagues of Professor Ted Aoki recollect his work and life as an educator and curricularist through their accounts of what it is like to venture forth with him in a shared world of education, as it is lived and made visible through questioning. Werner gives an account of how he interpreted Ted's writing and teaching:

> Teaching and learning represent a journey of interpreting and of being interpreted, the route clarified through the backward glance to where one was. This journey has an openness that allows new possibilities to come into being, while at the same time grounded in each participant's own historicity and professional story. As such, this journey always covers the terrain of personal struggle with one's own (or other's) assumptions (and implications) as these come into view. (Aoki 1987, 24–25)

Since I seem to find myself forever present in the metaphor of journey, these words have a particular calling power for me as I reread my words written and voiced at last year's AERA presentation with this group. I described my participation in this group as a journey with a sense of struggle, in which I experienced the right amount of tension—pulling me from reliance on my newly found language of phenomenology to an expression of me *in* the world created by this language (Hultgren 1987). In that paper I was also describing my search for a method of questioning to preserve an openness to being and my turning to Gadamer to help make sense of the essence of such questioning.

As a master of this art of questioning, Ted raised a question which immediately startled me and served to call forth a deeper questioning of the place from which I speak as I pursue my dwelling in the question: *In your understanding of phenomenology and hermeneutics, would you say that your understanding is stronger because of your technological background?* I was truly *caught* by the question. It seemed to turn my understanding upside down. My first inclination was to want to say *no*—that it had in fact served to impede my understanding. But then I began to feel the opening created by the question and my response followed at a first level of immediate reflection:

> Pause... Hmmmmm. That is interesting. I've never thought about it. Right off I think maybe what it allowed me to do and still allows me to do is that I have such a passion from having been in that technical orientation and recognizing what it was doing for me and *to* me and the way it had encapsulated me. Struggling so hard to get out of that and knowing what it was like to be there has generated that passion—to be able to maybe in a sense run away from it. But it also allows the seeing of some of the dimensions maybe of the concrete, and in that sense maybe the technical enriches the interpretive and the interpretive allows us to see what the technical is doing. So there's maybe a tension between those two that in a sense is enriching as well.

As with other persons experiencing the productive silence of Ted's questioning, I have come to realize the importance of that single question for me, and it is here in the direction of that initial question last year that I will dwell now as I reenter the conversation through my writing, as Carson suggests a response to Ted's questioning: "Silence. Reconsideration. And now a renewed conversation with a keener awareness of the language of the talk" (1987, 9).

Hearing the Silence in the Turning

I am mindful of the silence I experienced after being stopped short by this question. The question pointed me to my grounding, from which I was seeking to run away or throw off. I have rephrased the question so as to enter into the spaces I have kept silent far too long, as I now attempt that "backward glance" to where I have been as I am thrown back on the question: *How has my being-in-the-world which has been technologically determined allowed for a deeper revealing of my being, as a turning to hermeneutic phenomenology has been my mediation of new meaning through language, particularly poetic or narrative language?* As Ricoeur (1984) suggests, "The task of hermeneutics is to charter the unexplored resources of the to-be-said on the basis of the already-said" (p. 25). His interest is in creating meaning from a common heritage, "to receive a tradition and re-create it poetically to signify something new" (p. 26).

In seeking to create meaning from my technological heritage in this manner, I am reminded of Heidegger's questioning of technology, wherein in such questioning, he seeks to prepare a free relationship to it (1977b). He suggests that the relationship will be free if it opens our human existence to the essence of technology. If we can respond to its essence, we are able to experience the technological within its own bounds, and as he also suggests, we will never be able to experience its essence if we evade it, but rather we become chained to the technological in our denial of it. As I recall to memory my attempt last year to run as fast as I could from the *Ideas as Food* and *Weaving a Tapestry* metaphors, I reexperience how such a denial continues to keep me chained to the technological, and despite my *turn* to phenomenological knowing, my being-in-the-world remains concealed. I hear van Manen's caution: "If we simply try to ignore what we already know, we may find that the presuppositions persistently creep back into our reflections. It is better to make explicit our understanding . . . not to try to forget them again, but rather to *turn* this knowledge against itself— thereby exposing its shallow or concealing character" (1984, 46).

I am now caught by the language of *turning,* in my own writing, and in the writing of others informed by phenomenology. Aoki speaks of a call for "re-turning, a turning around, a turning of our thoughts again and again upon ourselves" (in Pinar 1987, 12). I am reminded also of the question asked of me from our group: "What is it that drew you to your phenomenological *turning* and orientation?" Van Manen (1984) suggests that every phenomenological project is driven by a commitment of turning to an abiding concern. Before proceeding further, I must look deeper into the meaning of turning, and for that illumination I go back to Heidegger, this time discovering a new essay I had not previously read, "The Turning." As he writes about the essence of technology (essence meaning coming to presence), he describes it as enframing, whereby being denies its own coming to presence—that is, the danger of technology. But, as he also suggests, where this danger exists, there is also a "saving power"—the concealed essence that is ever susceptible of turning:

> The turning of the danger comes to pass suddenly. In this turning, the clearing belonging to the essence of Being suddenly clears itself and lights up. This sudden self lighting is the lightning flash ... When, in the turning of the danger, the truth of Being flashes, the essence of Being clears and lights itself up. Then the truth of the essence, the coming to presence, of being, turns and enters in. (1977b, 44)

The recent screen play of Kundera's (1984) novel, *The Unbearable Lightness of Being*, brought this out very vividly to me. As people were lulled into not asking questions by the totalitarian "kitsch" that pervaded the then Soviet-occupied Prague of 1968, and the "escape to" country of freedom, Switzerland, the denial of freedom was especially pronounced with those who acquiesced to the given without capacity to look at things as if they could be otherwise. As the themes of power, sexuality, morality, life, death, and responsibility interacted with increasing intensity, the "lightning flash" announced itself for me in the question posed by the doctor's wife after his repeated episodes with other women: "How can you make love without being in love?" Silence ... Reconsideration. "A question is like a knife that slices through the stage backdrop and gives us a look at what lies behind it" (Kundera 1984, 250). What does it mean to make? What does it mean to be? What brings about the turning from one form of existence to another? In what manner has my technological background of a "making" nature interfered with my realization of "being"? In what manner has it helped to bring about the turning for me?

Turning (Old English *tyrnan*) is a verb of extensive sense development, the basic notions of which are rotation and deviation from a course. As I began to retrace the first tugs at my sense of turning, my deviation from a technological course, my thoughts raced back to my student teaching experience, which had been recently recalled to me as I discovered a long-buried paper I had written at the time as a reflection on that experience:, *What Is Teaching to Francine Holm?* A return to that experience twenty years ago reveals a flicker of the beginning of the turning, but possibly only a half turning—not far enough. However, the tension was being experienced, in a sense, between the "making" and in "being" as the following excerpts bring forth:

> The Francine Holm that started student teaching eight weeks ago was unaware of the problems she would encounter that would

play such a vital role in producing a change in her personality and self-perception.

Teaching is guiding, directing, stimulating, assisting students so that they will learn—will change in a desired way. But first of all, before I could accomplish this, I myself had to make a change in a desired way—understanding and acceptance of myself. An essential function of good education is to help the growing student to know himself and to grow in healthy attitudes of self-acceptance. I as a teacher could not make much headway in understanding others unless I first understood myself... I realized that I was very anxious, actually very scared of the school situation where I was teaching. I was, in a sense, residing on an island between what had been and what was yet to come... There were a number of factors that contributed to the ineffectiveness on my part. The anxiety I felt caused me to hide behind this screen—looking at the students but not really seeing them individually... The problem of discipline with them seemed almost uncontrollable. I realize that this problem was patterned and set forth by a number of other factors on my part, but many of them didn't really know what respect was—they hadn't learned it at home. Through discussion with my supervising teacher and getting to know the students better, I could pinpoint those students which were the leaders of class disruption. I then made out a seating chart to alleviate some of the talking. This did give me better control in the classroom. I didn't carry plans through to their completion. I was just plain too meek. I had this brought to my attention quite vividly one day. One girl raised her hand and asked if she could make a suggestion. She proceeded to say, "Miss Holm, I think it would help if you would raise your voice at us and show us that you mean business. You're too nice; we need to be yelled at once in awhile to bring us back to order..."

My first lessons were quite lecture-oriented, so I searched for more effective ways of involving the students, as active participation by a learner is preferable to passive reception when learning. I decided to try more lab work for learning experiences. This worked especially well for the girls in Interiors. Working on their floor plans in class encouraged them to share their ideas with their classmates, and with me as well. They came to respect my ideas more, and I could check their daily progress. It also helped me to get to know them as individuals, by roaming about from student to student... My experience in this area is more limited in comparison to other areas, such as foods and clothing. I was left with free choice of what I would have them do, in a sense, but the school's curriculum for home economics stressed motor skills; so combined with that pressure and also the girls' wanting very much to do floor plans, I decided to have them draw their own plans using magazines for ideas... Now I feel justified in having them draw the plans, because the satisfactions the girls experienced from their completed plans was a great reward for them and for me as well... Just as it is within an interpersonal setting that one acquires most of the attitudes involved in one's view of oneself, so it is likely that only in an interpersonal setting can a person be helped to come to grips with some of the meanings of these attitudes... Through the more personal and informal structure of these labs I came to realize that, no matter how perfect one's knowledge of content is, it won't reach the students unless the students are truly motivated and have fun learning.

In my foods class, the girls failed to see the purpose of making out work schedules; they just wouldn't write them. So I let them go into one lab without making out a work schedule, and as I anticipated, it turned out to be chaos—so the next day during evaluation of the meal they admitted they needed a plan. I tried to help them realize that six girls working in a kitchen to prepare one meal is quite different from one girl doing it alone... When I wanted to present new content, I found that it worked best to use an informal group, having something to display, such as in a demonstration, and wherein they could try it... I feel I have to defend my choice of content for the foods class on cakes... The lesson was planned as an experiment—not just for performance of skill at making cakes, but rather for understanding the method in relation to the chemistry of ingredients... I was expanding on a familiar concept to awaken new interest and ideas...

Looking back on the entire eight weeks as a whole, I feel the most satisfactory experience with myself in overcoming the curtain between the students and myself that I started at the beginning. It's difficult for one to change one's personality in a period of eight weeks, because it involves many things... To feel for others, to feel *with* others, it is essential that the teacher draw upon her own capacity for feeling. And this she can do only if she respects her feelings and is at home with them, feeling free to express them and accept them as fighting the struggle within myself of trying to be more openly expressive than I formerly was capable of being... The last day when the students gave me parties, I couldn't resist the temptation to respond to the girl's request that I raise my voice and yelled, "CLASS!" The entire class jumped and looked up and they really broke up, including myself. I received applause from the students, and the girl who made the suggestion and I exchanged winks and she said, "Well I didn't believe you could do it." They knew and I knew then that a true communication of human warmth and understanding was being portrayed. The cut crystal vase they gave me will always be treasured by me as a symbol of the student-teacher relationship we achieved through much effort on my part, and theirs too.

Revisiting this experience through my words written twenty years ago has been like meeting a ghost of my past that brings forth a striking confrontation with memories lived—too painful to remember, but also too painful to forget—distant but not distant—the past but yet *now.* The stark realization is that I began my pursuit of this ghost before the ink was dry on those reflections twenty years ago and which I am still in pursuit of today, as Ted's question prompted me to confront. What is this ghost and in what manner has it revealed itself to me? It has to do with the struggle to overcome a professional identity that has been technologically determined and the feelings of inferiority resulting from a profession that has been devalued because of its technological image.

Pursuing the Ghost of "Doing" to Allow a Place for "Being": Patterning that Begins Transcendence

Likening my experience to the pursuit of a ghost as an opening to make sense of my struggle came about in my search to understand the question in which I presently dwell, and the reading I have done to help bring me insights for looking anew on what has been:

> You look at where you're going and where you are and it never makes sense, but then you look at where you've been and a pattern seems to emerge. And if you project forward from that pattern, then sometimes you can come up with something. (Persig 1974, 149)

It is Persig's book, *Zen and the Art of Motorcycle Maintenance,* that has served as a very recent resource for me to gain deeper insights into the dialectic tension I am seeking to understand between technological and hermeneutic ways of knowing and being. He is also in pursuit of a ghost—the ghost of rationality itself as he lives out his search through Phaedrus, pursuing the ghost of rationality because he wanted to "wreak *revenge* on it, because he felt he himself was so shaped by it. He wanted to free himself from his own image. He wanted to destroy it because the ghost was what *he* was and he wanted to be free from the bondage of his own identity" (Persig 1974, 75).

The bondage of my identity that I have felt so stifled by, that emerged in my student teaching reflections, and that continues to rear its unwanted presence, is that of being identified by what I *do* rather than what I *am*. I turned to laboratory experiences in the belief that the *doing* was what fostered learning, but at the same time *justified* turning to those experiences by what occurred there—the presencing of our *selves with* each other through the laboratory encounter. There was an image I had of laboratory work as negative—the equipment— the products made—that focused on low level or "mindless" skills. In a sense I was both dependent on these modes of knowing and yet reject- ing of them—which served to create a dislike for technical knowing, and maybe even more significantly, covered up the potential for enter- ing into a free relationship with it. I also experienced the bondage of schools themselves calling teachers to be disciplinarians—the expecta- tion of control in classrooms—that called forth a mode of existence that did not bring out my own authentic way of relating. At the time of student teaching I saw my "lack of control" as a flaw that had to be overcome, not questioning what that way of relating was calling upon me to do. Resisting that control and trying to preserve my authentic way of being was experienced as a tension, although I was unable to name it as such at the time.

The ghost of other voices beginning at this early time and carried on through present day continue their imposed view of a "doing" pro- fession:

"You're a home economics education major?
Why do you need a degree for that?"
"You're a home economist are you? Well, what do you do—cook or sew?"
"You're a Ph.D. in home economics education? Boy! I'll bet you can make a mean loaf of bread!"
"It should make me nervous having you over for dinner being you are a home economist."

Other experiences shared in conversation from a home economics teacher reveal a similar imposition of definition:

"We're considered a practical subject in the sense of a product to show—having the muffins, the aprons, the doing of laundry, dishes, etc. And the students say—I figured I could miss your class. It's just home economics."
"My college was an extension of high school. We went into the labs—I knew how to make my own mayonnaise, I knew how to cut up a chicken; I could give a bang-up demonstration on how to do something."

"My next principal liked home economics, but she liked us because
we provided the doughnuts and punch for visiting people."

Feelings that continue to surface in relation to home economics and
this way of knowing clearly reveal tones of embarrassment, second
class, not intellectual, mechanical, not valued, apologetic, and devoid of
being. Is it any wonder that one would want to run from these associations? I became dedicated to my *journey,* then, in a sense, because of
doubting the goals of my profession and an imposed or received view
of it from society. Similar journeys with other home economists have
led us together in the examination and reconceptualization of home
economics curriculum from a phenomenological-critical perspective.
But the voices of the past ghosts are still very haunting. If we do not
run from them, but rather enter into them, maybe the questions can be
thrown back upon themselves—and the technical may also be revealed
with a different understanding.

Mu—Un-asking the Question to Re-enter the Experience

In seeking to move away from the contrast of "doing" and "being," as if
one can really take place without the other, I recall Persig's (1974) use
of the Japanese *mu,* meaning no thing—not yes, not no. *Mu* calls for a
reasking of the question because the context of the question is too
small for the truth of the answer; the answers are found beyond classi-
fications of dualistic thinking in yes-or-no terms. Rather than confining,
then, a technological way of knowing to that of a doing nature, we
broaden the context to establish a freer relationship to it. A *mu* state
reveals other possibilities, and the way to see those possibilities might
come through questioning that would help establish renewed contact
with original experience. To be aware of the structures of experiencing
the technological may provide some clues as to the way in which we
might reorient ourselves to the doing so that being shines through. I
begin with a series of questions:

> How do I understand a technological way of knowing?
> In what manner do I relate to that which I seek to know?
> What is my place in this knowing or where do I find my *self* and
> the self of others in such knowing?
> What language expresses my coming to know?
> In what manner has knowing that is technological structured my
> relationship with the world?
> In what manner has a phenomenological way of knowing freed me
> to create a different way of interacting in the world?

To enter these questions more fully, a naming—and then a possibly a renaming—of the language that calls forth this experience and understanding of the technological might serve to recreate the technical for a different understanding.

Reunderstanding the Technical: Making as Cultivating Being (Dwelling)

Heidegger (1977b) has said that words show the being of that which they speak and that they point to something beyond themselves. When I think about what language stands out to me as most reflective of a technical way of knowing, I first bring to mind "how-to" language: skills-learning, ordering, step-by-step procedures, functions, how something operates or works, products, equipment, *doing* something, hands-on experiences, laboratory learning, demonstration, method, performance, technique. In a sense, these are the words of other people—those who would describe a *conceptualization* of the technical. Those who might follow what Persig (1974) calls "spectator manuals" (how-to-do-it instructions) for completing a technical task, would experience teaching and learning such a skill as if the equipment or procedures to complete it or the product completed were isolated in time and space from the world—having no connection or relationship to you, or you having no relationship to them. Caring and relating are absent from this spectator posture. But from where does this posturing come? Is it inherent in technology and technological knowing itself, or is it in the use we make of it? We might also question in whose interest is it that professions become devalued and people in them disempowered because of an association with the technological? *Has that been my real struggle: Wanting to restore a sense of caring to that which we relate technologically?* Having experienced what is wrong in a "seeing" that overlooks the person (that might have been an imposed set of lenses from outside the technological rather than from the sight which might be possible from within the technological) allows me to *care.* If I care, I am more open to experience the "readiness-to-hand" of equipment or technology (Heidegger 1962), how it connects persons together in their relation with its use. We might also question, then, how technology and technical knowing have been separated from caring—from art—doing from being—allowing shame and denial to overcome pride. What has been covered up in the process? Is that why I always seem to be digging (the archeologist that Mary describes me as) to uncover that which has been silted over?

If technology or technique can be viewed in terms of the derivative upon which it rests, *techne,* a skilled and thorough knowing—a mode of bringing forth presencing, a mode of revealing—how might some of the language that has grown out of the technological be re-created to show the possibility of a different relationship in the world? In the process of reawakening language to rediscover the meaning of being-in-the-world, how does the process of hermeneutic reflection allow for the shining through of the being that is there in understanding technology and a way of knowing it or meeting it as it is lived? As Heidegger suggests, it is language that reveals the essence of something—provided we respect the essence of the language itself (1977b).

The idea of *making* seems to underlie much of the language that has evolved out of our attempts to conceptualize the technological. What, then, does it mean to make? The Old English word *macian,* or German *machen,* means 'to bring into existence or cause to be.' As one thinks, then, of the person who makes (maker) the creator, or manufacturer or the poet as translated from the Greek, *poetes,* we connect the person doing the making with the making. When I make something, what do I do and how do I experience the making—in what manner do I relate to that which I am making and to others who may be gathered together through that which is made? Let's take that "mean loaf of bread" as an example of "a making." I will have a product at the end of my making, but as I am engaged in the making I anticipate the pleasure it brings to others: it draws me close to those for whom I care. It is not so much, then, what the product is, but rather the meaning that it has for me in the making and the connection it brings with others in the receiving of that which is made with care. What other forms of making go into that which might be called "home-making"? Typically we consider the making of physical products such as meals, the making of purchases, the making of spaces of living in the home, the making of clothing or clothing repairs; but we also have the making of relationships, the making of values, the making of children, the making of goals and aspirations for living, and the making of moral judgments in the interests of those who are family members. Each form of making may have a different end in view, and yet there is a relationship that occurs which is not merely a means-end continuum. To Heidegger (1977a) again I have turned for that illumination in his essay, "Building—Dwelling—Thinking."

Bauen, meaning 'to build' in German, comes from the Old High German word for building, *buan,* meaning 'to dwell.' If building is seen only as a *means* to dwelling as Heidegger suggests, the essential relation between the two is missed, that is, "to build is in itself already to dwell" (Heidegger 1977a, 324). In connecting this relation to *making,* building for Heidegger is seen as a making or constructing of products, but also as a cultivating—a nurturing. Both modes of building are forms of dwelling. In tracing the etymology of *bauen* to its original speaking, in the sense of how far the essence of dwelling reaches, Heidegger shows that "*bauen* to which *bin* belongs answers: *ich bin, du bist* (which means) I dwell, you dwell" (p. 325). To make something, then, is not merely a means for some end, because in the making, I already dwell—I am. The question of building or making, then, is more than a technical concern. As Burch (1986) interprets this sense of building, he suggests that to build genuinely is to construct a home, a place where human beings can be at home in the world. The "making of a home," then, as seen in this light casts a new meaning on the things made and the persons making them: making is a dwelling, and in dwelling I am at home in the world with others.

The tension I have experienced around my denial of the technological might be an expression of not really allowing myself to dwell in it—to be at home in it. I asked the question last year: What is it like to live a metaphor of one's own choice as opposed to somebody else's imposition? My journey might well be, then, a search for dwelling—a place where I feel at home, and my turnings have been paths *chosen* in a new language (phenomenology), which have helped me to restore the meaning and presence of that which I have uncovered: *me* in my writing, speaking, and being. I am drawn to Ted Aoki's (1987) reflections on the "me" in his story—a me reunderstood that points away from the "I" rather than to it—a pointing to the other (otherness) which possibly grants our being. If I loosen the devaluing hold that an imposed metaphor has on my ego self—I, in what sense can the "me" be freed to experience otherness and to dwell and be at peace within that which is freed up? Is the "saving power" really, then, the journey—the discovery of "otherness" as one moves forward, experiencing the tensions between leaving and entering—the turnings of the paths with others as they present themselves? To be at peace—to dwell and to be at home in the world—does not mean to dissolve the tension, but rather to lend a helping hand to being as the way traveled is thought about. Maybe it is as Persig says: "Sometimes it's a little better to travel than arrive" (1974, 103).

References

Aoki, T. (1987). In receiving, a giving: A response to the panelists' gifts. *The Journal of Curriculum Theorizing, 7* (3), 67–88.

Burch, R. (1986). Confronting technophobia: A topology. *Phenomenology + Pedagogy, 4* (2), 3–21.

Carson, T. R. (1987). Teaching as curriculum scholarship: Honoring Professor Ted Tetsuo Aoki. *The Journal of Curriculum Theorizing,* 7 (3), 7–10.

Heidegger, M. (1962). *Being and time.* New York: Harper & Row.

Heidegger, M. (1977a). Building dwelling thinking. In D. F. Krell (Ed.), *Martin Heidegger: Basic writings.* New York: Harper & Row, 320–339.

Heidegger, M. (1977b). *The question concerning technology.* New York: Harper & Row.

Hultgren, F. (1987). *My journey from knowing to being in phenomenology: Caught in the language and pursuit of method.* Paper presented at the annual meeting of the American Educational Research Association, Washington, DC, April.

Kundera, M. (1984). *The unbearable lightness of being.* New York: Harper & Row.

Persig, R. M. (1974). *Zen and the art of motorcycle maintenance.* New York: Bantam.

Pinar, W. F. (1987). "... Unwanted strangers in our own homeland": Notes on the work of T. Aoki. *The Journal of Curriculum Theorizing,* 7 (3), 11–21.

Ricoeur, P. (1984). I: The creativity of language. In R. Kearney (Ed.), *Dialogues with contemporary continental thinkers.* Dover, NH: Manchester University Press, 17–36.

van Manen, M. (1984). Practicing phenomenological writing. *Phenomenology + Pedagogy,* 2 (1), 36–69.

Werner, W. (1987). The text and tradition of an interpretive pedagogy. *The Journal of Curriculum Theorizing,* 7 (3), 22–33.

Ted in Conversation with Francine

In recent years, my conversations with you and the other members of the study group crested and waned with the coming and going of the annual AERA conferences. So it is that my memory of the conversations related to your study group's papers seems to be in layered horizons, each layer embedded with a symposium theme that appeared on AERA conference programs:

> 1988.—Re-searching the Meaning of Metaphors That Guide Curriculum Practice: Speaking, Reflecting, Writing
>
> 1987.—Conversation Across Disciplines: Hermeneutic Priority of the Question for Interpretation of Curriculum Text
>
> 1984.—Curriculum Inquiry as Being: Reflections of a Study Group Encountering Each Other Through Interpretive Inquiry

I sense in the texture of these layers as a whole two subtexts: a journeying in the question of what it is to come together in dialog, and a journeying in the question of what it is to study about interpretive research while becoming engaged in a hermeneutic of experiences in conversation.

Now, at this moment as I allow the horizonal themes to recede, what surges forth are the texts of your set of papers, where I am called by your wordings into the language of your lived experiences.

Theme 1: Struggling to Understand What It Is to Lead

I know that you, Francine, committed as you are to the primacy of dialogical "we-ness," struggled with the question of what it is to lead. In your first paper, "Finding Our Own Voices," you lived in that struggle to understand what it is like to lead and to tactfully act. You wrote of "leading" as embodied "holding . . . in check" and as "withholding," displaying in these words an attunement to how, in belonging to the group, you tried to be responsibly responsive to others.

You continued to linger in your concern for the meaning of what it is to lead humanly. I find this reflected in your 1988 paper, "Destining of Being Through Technological Knowing." Here, you disclosed your understanding of leadership more fully worded in the language of "otherness that grants our being." Such a saying shows deep concern for how "we-ness" can be allowed to grow intactly. You seem to be deeply conscious of what Heidegger calls "the event of appropriation," a realm wherein in belonging-together-with-others central is the gesture of letting be, of letting things come to be on their own—a gesture some call "enownment." It seems to be that "we-ness" within enownment is more than a fusion of horizons but a "we-ness" that insistently remains open to openness.

I am excited by your transformed seeing that allows us to return to the originary meaning of *education.* Etymologically, at the source of *education* is *e* [out] + *ducare* [to lead] (a leading out), suggesting the possibility of enownment, a coming into one's own becomingly in the realm of possibilities.

Theme 2: In-Dwelling More Sufficiently Where You Already Are

For another theme in our conversation, I recall our conversation following the presentation of your 1987 paper, "My Journey From Knowing to Being in Phenomenology." You told us, then, of your effort to turn from being in the language of Heidegger and Gadamer to the language of the ground floor. Do you remember this conversation?

Ted: You said, Francine, that you were keeping company with Heidegger and Gadamer at the level of "cloud nine" and that you are attempting to move to the ground level of lived experiences. You said you left Heidegger and Gadamer behind. My interest focuses on "leaving." When you leave anything behind, is not whatever you leave behind still hanging on with you? If so, is not what you left behind a part of where you now are?

Francine: I find a lot of complexity wrapped up in that question. It has to do, I think, with both trying to enter and also leaving something that was a prior experience. In my own situations it involves throwing off the technical language of my discipline, home economics, and turning to a new language. First, I entered this new language at a superficial "cloud nine" level, and later I sought it at the ground level... I see it as a leaving of a prior orientation (the technical) and entering a new orientation through a new language that allows me to see differently. For me, this involved throwing off somebody else's language and entering through my own. I found myself in a vulnerable place.

Ted: Dwelling as you say in a vulnerable place, would you say that your new understanding of your place is "stronger" because you had undergone the experience within the technical orientation which you are now leaving behind?

This last question became for you the beginning of your final paper. Fittingly, you interpreted the call of the question as follows:

How has my being-in-the-world, which has been technologically determined, allowed for deeper revealing of my being, as a turning to hermeneutic phenomenology has been by my mediation of new meaning through language, particularly poetic or narrative language?

In and through this question, you entered an opening that the question has allowed, and as I see it your living in the question is indeed the vibrancy of your text in the last paper (AERA Conference 1988). My reading of the text is not so much a story of a movement from X to Y (from the technological orientation of home economics curriculum to the phenomenological), nor is it a mere disavowal of the old, but rather it is a returning to that place which people in their eagerness to turn away tend to hurry over. I see your turning as a paradox—both a distancing and a coming near to a place that is often difficult to see because it is so near.

This turning is reminiscent of Heidegger, who in his later years resolved to move away from his own metaphysical enframement and asked, "Where to?" To his own question, he answered, Where we already are; where we do not reside sufficiently as yet where in reality we already are (Heidegger 1969).

I am fascinated by your portrayal of your own dwelling place—your "home on earth," you called it—a place that openly acknowledges the presence of your existential past wherein you lived a life oriented to technique, a place that overcomes your own past denials and disavowals, a place where by turning your understanding against itself allowed light to fall more fully on your present dwelling place "where in reality you already reside."

When the draft of your paper reached me, my son and I were engaged in discussing Kundera's *The Unbearable Lightness of Being* (1984). I immediately shared with him your concern of how in your curriculum situation, there is occurring an impoverishment of life through the "oblivion of Being," as Heidegger would say.

And so returning as you did to your own curriculum area, you without wincing moved to what John Caputo in *Radical Hermeneutics* called for, "restoring life to its original difficulty, and not to betray it with metaphysics" (p. 1). You struggled simultaneously with two questions: "What does it mean to make? What does it mean to be?" And in the tensionality of difference that grants a rupture, you dwelt in difference as difference, in the *mu* of not yes, not no.

What I think is indeed radical (in its authentic meaning) about your turning is your living in the turning that knows the humus, the dwelling place of humans.

How appropriate it is, then, that you in living in the opening refused to bring closure by a synthetic fusing of horizons which brings about an end to tension. It is in this refusal that I see a fullness of enownment in your words, "To be at peace—to dwell and to be at home in the world—does not mean to dissolve the tension, but rather to lend a helping hand to being as the way traveled is thought about."

You have led me, Francine, to that inspirited realm where curriculum is being. And I almost feel that I am inhabiting a place where in the neighborhood is the presence of *mu*—no word—all silence.

References

Caputo, J. (1987). *Radical hermeneutics.* Bloomington, IN: Indiana University Press.

Heidegger, M. (1969). The principle of identity. In *Identity and difference.* New York: Harper & Row, 23–41.

Kundera, M. (1984). *The unbearable lightness of being.* New York: Harper & Row.

Mary's Voice

I grew up in the far northwest, about as close to the edge of the country as one could be and still live in a town. I had a sense of being an observer, on the edge, looking and thinking. But I also grew up in a large, secure family which provided me with a place to be and belong, a feeling of "we-ness."

Being in this group has in some ways re-created the feelings of these formative years—simultaneous sense of being a "we" and of being on the edge, observers and thinkers.

I came east to college, more observing, some connecting. Majoring in history gave me a sense of place in the larger world; focusing on English history elongated my biocultural roots.

Like many young women of the time, I did not give much thought to a career. However, also like others, I found that elementary teaching was compatible, even convergent at many points, with raising young children.

Then through various forces such as restlessness, graduate work, and family changes, I took other teaching posts—nursery school, community college, the university. And I've taught many workshops for other teachers as well.

I reflect on these teaching times and places, and I appreciate the observation that what you actually teach is yourself. A humbling thought.

I do not completely understand this text I teach, but there seem to be some irreducibles: an elemental belief in freedom, a desire for grace, and a yearning for community.

What Are We Interpreting? The "Data" Problem

*This piece reflects a struggle to move between paradigms—to
realize the implications of moving: for thinking, for talking,
for being.*

*For me there was a sense of relief in the move because I did
not like reductionist thinking. It always leaves out something
and its conclusions are too constructed—something in me
always wants that left-out part, perhaps even more than the
included part.*

We all know what data are. That's what you get when you do research
and you analyze it and find out something. But what are data in interpretive research? Is *data* even an appropriate word to use?

> *Data* indicated to me something that you act upon; something that
> has been collected... From the phenomenological orientation,
> that's not what we're doing. We have something that we're inter-
> preting, but it's really more in the form of text. And text is not
> similar to data. (Francine)

Jane objected: "Text doesn't exist out there, in the world where you
come to, it's constructed. But there is something out there." Do data
represent the "something out there" in a way that text does not? Yes,
for they come from a look out there through a lens carefully and scrupulously *narrowed* to avoid confounding and contaminating. And text:
what does it come from? It comes from a look out there with a lens
carefully and scrupulously *widened* to include as much as possible, to
see and seize a totality, and render it in a language that others might
share what has been seen.

Using Texts for This Inquiry

In our group, we began with an interest in text and varying degrees of
faith. We began writing texts, short essays about parts of our lives and
experiences. Then we would interpret these texts. Soon we began tape-

recording our meetings and realized that the transcripts of these were texts, too. Some of us laughed at this; we were very serious and thinking that interpretive inquiry was somewhere out there as a thing to be approached and studied; then we realized it was right there, in what we said to one another about the written texts and research problems.

As each situation in life is different, each interpretive inquiry is different. As Jessie said, what you learn is "the road you travel by to get where you went." The first step on our road was simple enough. We each wrote a theme, then paired up to share the theme. Each of us tried to interpret the other's writing by making groupings of ideas and tried to grasp the total meaning of the essay. Then we told the other person what we'd found, achieved a consensual validation of the meaning; and shared this with the whole group. As we went on, we all read all themes and tried either to pull commonalities out of them or to allow themes to emerge from the collection.

We began hesitantly. Sharing an interpretation with the theme's author, we would say, "Does this sound right?" "Is that what you meant?" We became more confident as we came to understand the subject, our inquiring selves, more. We became able to read pages of text and extract themes from them without fearing (too much) committing the injustice of misunderstanding one another. Even so, the challenge inherent in interpretation has been constant; Louise noted after several months:

> I'll have to admit to much feeling of personal inadequacy in attempts to make sense of what other persons are saying.
>
> Perhaps the difficulties and dangers inherent in interpretive inquiry account for the popularity of the positivistic approach to research.

Guidelines in Interpreting Text

Looking at our work, I see we had two implicit guidelines in our approach to text. First, we were whole-person oriented, not fragmented. Jane said, to general agreement, "We can't fragment children. Those horrible divisions—physical, emotional, cognitive." In this same spirit, we did not fragment one another: We assumed persons were speaking, rather than cognitive or affective entities. Second, we assumed that we could make sense out of what we were doing. We were seeking to learn, to study, to communicate, and that oriented us in a reasoning and reasonable way. We had faith (that combination of surety and doubt) that we could be, were, knowledge-creators. This was the "faithfulness" that Barnard speaks of in Darroch and Silvers: We tried to be fully present to the inquiry, and in that lay rigor (1982, 37).

Achieving Validation of Interpretations

After reading and reflecting on a text to obtain an understanding, how does one know if the understanding is reasonable, accurate? Two methods of consensual validation were used by us: one, the interpreter told the person studied what she had learned, and the studied person could agree, disagree, or amplify; and two, several persons would work on the same texts and pool their interpretations. After all, as Gadamer reminds us, a text does not have infinite possibilities. If we are open to its range of possibilities and aware of our own biases, we can reasonably hope to interpret text accurately.

The Challenges of Using Interpretively Gained Knowledge

Jana observed that it was difficult to report the kinds of knowledge gained from the interpretation:

> I read [dialog] journals and see in each exchange something of the Holy or the Mystery at the Center of the Universe. I can see it plain, right there, and yet when I turn to the paper I write, I do not speak of this presence.

Somehow, it is hard to fit into "the paper" with its external requirements.

The knowledge that teachers have from the experience of teaching, yet keep to themselves as inferior to scholarly research, is another indication of the difficulty of using this kind of knowledge.

Bringing this uncountable, individually held knowledge together into theory is another challenge. How does the private become public and synthesizable? Can our writing and talking with one another coalesce into theoretical understandings?

Praxis for Curriculum Planners

What does our experience with text in studying interpretive inquiry imply for those persons who are concerned with curriculum? At least two implications emerge.

First, text and curriculum are much alike. Just as text awaits interaction to become meaningful, so does curriculum. The teacher brings a part of the world to the student, but the student must interact with it to own it, to bring it to understanding. The student's understanding then influences subsequent curriculum. We move in a spiral of interactions.

Second, insofar as we who studied were able to decide how and what we studied, and to make meaning of it that we valued, it seems to me that teachers and students working in classrooms are similarly capable. Teachers and children have enormous curriculum-creating capabilities that perhaps we would do well to acknowledge.

References

Darroch, V., and V. Silvers (1982). *Interpretive human studies: An introduction to phenomenological research.* Washington, DC: University Press of America.

Gadamer, H-G. (1975). *Truth and method.* New York: Crossroad.

Living Off the Inheritance

*In this part I chose to focus on the aspect of my professional
life which seemed most distant from the professional lives of
the others because we in our presentation were seeking to be
interdisciplinary. As I think about it, I see that it, like my
previous paper, displays the effort to move between
paradigms. To move from being deterministic to being interpretive, but without losing things I valued.*

I have been struggling with finding a place for myself in the inheritance of science. I teach science education to preschool teachers—what
I teach is fragmented and truncated, and I have been worrying about
the fragmentation and truncation and I've been worrying about science itself. As our group has discussed our mutual and diverse endeavors, we have gravitated toward metaphors that enable us to elaborate,
illuminate, and occasionally celebrate. One of the metaphors inherent
in teaching is that of the inheritance—the conceived world that the
teacher seeks to bring to the student, the third party to the dialog. To
me, the inheritance of science is troublesome, flawed actually.

Science and technology dominate our age. I am fascinated by science, by its powers, its details, its confidence and range. But the approach to nature that comes down to us through science has been one
of domination and fragmentation—seeking to predict nature and to
break it into the smallest pieces, to probe inner secrets, to atomize.
Bacon used metaphors of sexual penetration in his enthusiasms for science's method. This drive to control nature through fragmenting it has
led to incredible disasters: pollution, nuclear wastes, and threatened an-
nihilation of nature. Nature has been turned inside out to devour itself
and ourselves as natural creatures as well. Surely this is a human endeavor gone wrong. Science is mind-boggling in its range: I have been
thrilled by the moon landing, the probes of space, the medical and ag-
ricultural advances, but even more I am chilled by the threats lingering,
shadowing, haunting these positive gains.

Evelyn Fox Keller, in her thoughtful *Reflections on Gender and
Science,* describes how the exclusion of women from the history of cre-

ating science has contributed to this dangerous situation. She thinks that a female Bacon would not have used the metaphor of sexual intercourse to represent the scientific endeavor. Perhaps nature would have been regarded as something to work with rather than to dominate. She cites the example of plant geneticist Barbara McClintock, who worked in a mode differing from the mainstream: While Watson and Crick were developing a model that would explain everything, that would take care of all cases (but eventually has proved not to), McClintock worked to understand individual differences, not to group all cases together, rather to know variety, and to believe that differences among cases show the way to understanding as much as similarities do. The messiness of biology versus the hard model aspirations of physics, the preeminent science. McClintock's work, long unappreciated but eventually highly regarded, shows that scientists can approach nature as a pluralistic whole, rather than as a phenomenon to be rigorously quantified and classified.

Science-the-inheritance sometimes seems to me to be a huge file cabinet jammed with vast numbers of file folders which are constantly increasing. It is a burden we carry around as we move from house to house, dipping into it for various purposes, ignoring most of it most of the time. Even if I were a practicing scientist, I would work in only a few files, because that is the nature of modern science—enormous specialization. Jessie asked me once, when we were discussing teaching, how I made connections for my students. I had to say that's one of the things I was struggling with. How to avoid flipping through the files.

Keller's book made me start a new file, marked with capital letters, "READ THIS AGAIN. THIS IS HOPEFUL." It encourages me in my desire to turn my face outward from the inheritance. The problem is, as Gadamer reminds us, that we are so imbued with our surroundings that our self-consciousness is but a dim flickering, that the prejudgments we absorb constitute the historical reality of our being far more than our individual judgments (1975, 245). Thus I may make the judgment that science as presently constituted is sending us all awry, but my being is permeated with the spirit of our age, which is the scientific-technological one.

Jessie and Diane often speak of being fence-sitters or being "behind," yet it seems to me that they are feeling the tension between their historical beings and their self-created beings. We are limited, but we do have some power to reinvent ourselves—we do. T. S. Eliot tells us in "Little Gidding" to continue to be explorers: "We shall not cease from exploration" (p. 39).

I want to explore other ways of looking at science. The feminist critique of science, exemplified by Keller and also sociologist Dorothy

Smith, provides such a way. Smith (1979) particularly speaks of the power of naming. What we name the world shapes how we see it. As women gain more power to name, we will gain new visions.

Words other than names also provide ways of regarding science. I looked into the etymology of *holistic* and was delighted to find that *holistic* and *holy* share the same Indo-European root, *kailo. Holy, wholeness, holistic, healthy*: all originated in the same root concept. And curiously in the German, Norse, and English languages, the same languages that nurtured the growth of the Euro-American scientific enterprise with its disastrous unwholeness, its relentless atomism, and resultant unhealthiness. The etymological unity of the sacred and the physical is very welcome to me.

I am fascinated by other cultures' approaches to science—tantalized by the ecological perspective of Native Americans, intrigued by ancient Egypt's synthesis, and I try to learn the lessons that will be relevant to our situation.

Fritz Capra's paralleling of modern physics and Eastern mysticism is relevant to my concerns: Capra thinks that modern physics and ancient philosophy agree on the essential organic harmony and unity in nature, although modern physicists do not realize the social implications of their theories. If nature is an organic unity, then we need new social and political structures to match.

I despair of having the psychic energy to master other cultural views but know they would probably cause my whole file cabinet to rock. Probably my existence.

Which brings me to another metaphor that our group lives with—that of the pilgrim. The science pilgrim travels the Himalayas in a snowstorm—towering mountains of information and a blizzard of new information constantly surrounding one. In much of my nonscience teaching, I do feel like a pilgrim, but not in science because pilgrims are on their way to known and hallowed spots. What hallowed spots can possibly lie at the end of our current road? I want to explore but not to know my destination, except by shape and essence. I rather like the idea of being a pioneer, staking a new spot to try planting shoots and seeds of ideas that seem helpful and hopeful. I want to work on restructuring knowledge—to make it more holy, holistic, and integrated. And when I teach teachers of young children, I want to share a nonfragmented knowledge of nature. Possibly, few would recognize it as science.

Diane gave us another metaphor, that of the quilt, pieced-together knowledge for our use. Yeats wrote about making his coat of old mythologies—can I call modern science that?—and how he abandoned it to "fools:"

let them take it,
For there's more enterprise
In walking naked.

W. B. Yeats
(*A Coat*)

I do not think I am up to walking naked. I want our old quilt trailing along over my shoulders. It too is an inheritance, it seems made by my mothers and sisters, unlike the file cabinet. It is stitched of the careful insights, the living experiences reflected into ideas, the weighed remark, the forgiving touch, the tolerance, the faithfulness, the small pleasures, moments saved and cherished. It is not used like the file cabinet but is always there, on the back of the chair or the foot of the bed. Homely, like home in Louise's phrasing, and unique, it comforts this wondering sojourner.

References

Capra, F. (1975). *The Tao of physics.* New York: Bantam.

Eliot, T. S. (1943). "Little Gidding" In *Four Quartets.* New York: Harcourt Brace Jovanovich, p. 39.

Gadamer, H-G. (1975). *Truth and method.* New York: Crossroad.

Keller, E. F. (1985). *Reflections on gender and science.* New Haven, CT: Yale University Press.

Smith, D. (1979) A sociology for women. In J. A. Sherman & E. T. Beck (Eds.), *The Prism of Sex Essays in the Sociology of Knowledge.* Madison, WI: University of Wisconsin Press.

Yeats, W. B. (1958). A coat. In *Collected poems.* New York: Macmillan, p. 125.

Knowing and Saying: Metaphors and Fragments

> *Our study of metaphor in our fourth year of being together gave me another focus. I began to look not at how they think and we think, but rather at how we all think, how we are all inveterately, ineradicably metaphorizers. In this I begin to lightly play with the implications for teaching that flow from this realization.*

As I often do, I had been thinking about Francine's metaphors of knowing. Geologic in content, they refer to uncovering layers of meaning, illuminating what was dark, penetrating depths.

In the kitchen, then, I was peeling a leek, and the activity presented itself akin to looking for truth. The heavy, dirty, coarse outer layers were cut away and discarded, the next layers were finer and cleaner, and finally the innermost layer appeared, clean, fresh, translucent, glowing. I saw, "Oh, this is what one looks for." What struck me is that the outermost layers resemble the hidden inner core, just as Plato's cave images resemble reality. What is true is not unknown to us: Our everyday experience is filled with coarse, outer leaves, suggesting the inner luminosity. The inner is the desirable, the remarkable part of existence. Gerard Manley Hopkins refers to "the dearest freshness deep down things" ("God's Grandeur").

Also inherent in this metaphor is the ideas of having to make some effort to get to the inner—to peel away, washing and trimming as one proceeds toward the center.

I felt shy about giving this metaphor to the group. It is so mundane, so homey, so associated with women's work, and trivializing. Gerhart and Russell (1984, 185) refer to the domestication of life as a source of discontent and state that metaphors can rescue large segments of human experience from such domestication, restoring mystery. And here, to the group, I present a metaphor laden with domesticity.

But here it was anyway. The fields of meaning for truth-seeking and for cleaning leeks had suddenly warped and overlapped each other, creating a new meaning.

Knowing Before Saying

There is an ontology of metaphor which is described by Gerhart and Russell (1984). The metaphor presents itself—one knows before one can say "Eureka!" Then the saying follows. For this metaphor, I told Diane what I had thought of, then I wrote it down, exploring it, holding it fast, developing it.

Through the writing and saying, others can share my metaphor. Then its fate is either to be used, perhaps to the point of solidifying and dying, or more likely it will not be used but will stay idiosyncratic.

I suspect this particular metaphor will probably stay idiosyncratic—leeks are too stinky, common, and large. From the same genre as "heaven in a grain of sand," it lacks the scope of that thought, from the highest to the humblest. "Truth in a Leek?" Well, all right if you insist. But it lacks a certain panache.

Idiosyncratic Metaphors Informing Teaching

The experience of seeing with the leek occurred, and so the metaphoric insight is part of me. It shows that one is always on the verge of things, something is always there ready to burst forth, not truly hidden but available to sight. There is light hidden just beyond, just behind— the inner truth is translucent. For me, the leek is more optimistic than the geological earth where the core isn't light but dense and heavy. This new metaphor encourages an optimism and expectancy. For teaching, that means that encounters with students are full of promise, even if wrapped coarsely.

Saying-before-Knowing—Searching for Metaphors in Conversation

As I thought about presenting this metaphor to the group, I anticipated encountering saying before knowing. I would make my private knowledge public, or available for conversation. I did not know exactly what would happen, but I thought about our numerous previous conversations and reflected that we have much saying before knowing or saying on the way to knowing.

Our conversations are often intense, energetic, and illuminating. We burn our matches freely, warming ourselves and lighting our way, until it is time to go home.

Conversation is rooted in the Latin verb *to turn*. That is a true root for us as our conversations turn rapidly from one person to another, from one idea to another. We all participate and in sharing the knowledge; each person's part is a fragment.

Afterward when one reads the transcripts of the conversations, they often seem flat and much meaning is lost. The words are residues of the event rather than the event as in writing. The non-words, the gestures, the intonations and intensities are lost, except in memory. The conversational event can be reconstructed, but only partially.

However, the memory of the event confirms the possibility of such events. Conversation, the turning, becomes a metaphor for unity, a temporary healing of the world's fragmentation, of the individual's solitary being.

Saying-before-Knowing Informing Teaching

Our conversations are like good class discussion with their warmth and flashes of illumination. Some students like discussions, some students dislike them. I wonder if the sense of alienation is increased among the dislikers as they observe the likers turning towards the topic and toward one another. When there is no participation, either mental or spoken, then no fields of meaning are being touched for that person, nor are they being developed. But mere participation is not what is wanted either. That can be Buber's third kind of speaking, the mutual monologs in which speakers are unconnected to one another (1955, 19)—they do not turn to one another but aim past one another. The voluntary turning-toward to what is needed. In such turning, there is the openness and questioning that leads into knowing.

Saying-with-Knowing through Writing

The saying from conversation or from thinking can turn into knowing through writing. Since writing is less immediate, lacking gesture and visual contact, it needs to be more graceful, tentacled, reaching out, seeking to attract another's mind. Writing enables a sustained presentation without the turns occasioned by another mind. But then, writing can be hard to talk about, as it is so developed and lengthy. Poetry with its fewer words is the ideal writing about which to converse.

Saying-through-Writing Informing Teaching

For the process of class discussions, writing can develop and solidify ideas. It can also be a way of encouraging students to stay with us as partners in conversation, a necessary condition of dialect (Gadamer 1975, 330). To have students write out a starting point for a discussion can be a way of helping them become aware of their individual horizons for interpreting a particular topic. To have them write after a discussion can help them pull together the fragments of ideas that they have grasped and integrate them. Sharing the writing with a few other students can help validate the thinking and encourage clarity as well.

Saying-with-Knowing to Guide Others and Self

Conversations that conclude in metaphor or are guided by metaphor are less fragmented. Francine's well-developed metaphors of layers of thought-meaning-truth with illumination have guided our group from the beginning, challenging us to go further, deeper—"deep meditation" was her directive to us for considering this set of papers. When Diane, reading somewhat hesitantly from a handwritten sheet, offered us a new metaphor, that of ourselves as quilt-makers, we all pulled it toward ourselves, changing our table into a quilting bee of pleasure in thought. We have shaped our discourse and experience with such metaphors.

Implications of Guiding Metaphors in Classroom Discussion

Our group conversations have shown me that an accepted metaphor can shape our conversations into a coherency. Perhaps it would be well to consider such guiding metaphors when beginning or developing class discussions, as ways of focusing or jelling the talk.

Implications of Guiding Metaphors in Being a Teacher

Another aspect of guiding metaphors is revealed in teaching. How I or any other teacher conceives metaphorically of self as teacher is heuristic. Using familiar metaphors such as gardening or transmitting (Scheffler 1960, 49–53) leads to predictable results. Conceiving oneself as a gardener, one expects blooming, a positive result, and also to do pruning, pinching off, and fertilizing. On the other hand, thinking of oneself as a transmitter, one expects reproduction of what is transmitted. Using a less familiar metaphor, that of a pilgrim (Westerhoff 1987), one expects both companionship and shared goals, as well as loneliness, uncertainty, and setbacks. Living in a metaphor can cause conflict for teachers if the metaphor runs counter to the one held by the school or system. Because I tend toward something my mother always warned me against, a mixed metaphor (specifically, I think of myself as a gardening pilgrim), I experienced severe conflict in a system that characterized itself as a "deliverer of instruction."

Revisiting Metaphors Previously Held

Earlier I referred to a work coauthored by a theologian and a physicist, Mary Gerhart and Allen Russell. In this they hold that metaphor is the basis of both religion and mature science. These fields are both quests for human understanding that arrive at their respective understandings in an identical fashion:

> The natural philosopher or theologian, in coming to know, encounters a limit-situation, experiences an ontological flash, has a disclosure experience, and in so doing, engages that which is entirely other. Here no doubt is possible. At this moment, there is a conviction, a sense of certainty that is not justified by any formal epistemological structure. Validation and verification come later as the new knowledge takes its place within our structure of understanding. But at that moment it is given.
>
> It is the commonness of that other, encountered in limit-experience, that makes the world of theology and the world of natural philosophy one. (1984, 168–69.)

This reconciling of these areas of inquiry, pointing the way to a healing of a centuries-old division is profoundly comforting to me. Gerhart and Russell describe how consensus is slow to arrive, that "common sense changes slowly, like the flow of a rock, and only as a result of constant pressure" (p. 178). Our group's geology metaphor returns, with new amplification.

Last year, I said and wrote how I felt trapped with my burdensome old file cabinets, the inheritance of science that I lugged around with me from house to house, always conceived of as rickety. Now I envision the inheritance in a radically different way, a sort of web of understanding spread over the world, glimmering, incandescent, oil on waters, in shifting patterns, capable of rupture and redesign, watered silk slanted into lamplight, old leaves rustling in the late afternoon light. Connecting, linking, irregular with irregularities, covering broad areas. I am becoming reconciled from this vision, and am happy again teaching what I can of this inheritance to others.

References

Buber, M. (1955). *Between man and man.* Boston: Beacon.

Gadamer, H-G. (1975). *Truth and method.* New York: Crossroad.

Gerhart, M. and A. Russell (1984). *Metaphoric process: the creation of scientific and religious understanding.* Fort Worth, TX: Texas Christian University Press.

Hopkins, G. M. (1953). God's grandeur. In *Poems and prose of Gerard Manley Hopkins.* Harmondsworth, England: Penguin, p. 27.

Scheffler, I. (1960). *The language of education.* Springfield, IL: Charles E. Thomas.

Westerhoff, J. H. (1987). The teacher as pilgrim. In F. Bolin & J. M. Falk (Eds.), *Teacher renewal: Professional issues, personal choices.* New York: Teachers College.

Ted in Conversation with Mary

Your three AERA papers assembled in the chapter that is your voice gather me into the folds of the world of conversations with your colleagues at the University of Maryland. I pause in my reading and linger in your remark in your autobiography that you grew up in the far northwest "about as close to the edge of the country as one could be and still live in a town." Your remark urges me to ponder about where I now am, here in British Columbia—north of the edge of your country, north of the northwest. I hear you saying, "Ted, that's somewhere beyond the edge." I'll tuck away a title for a possible sequel to this book. How about *Voices of Educators from Beyond the Edge?*

This distraction aside, I return to the point of your remark which was that the remembrance of the way your family provided you with "a place to be and belong," very akin, you said, to your living in conversation with your colleagues over the past four years—a place that came to be a place to be and belong.

In "Living Off the Inheritance," your 1987 AERA paper, you told us of your struggle with the question of how to understand the place of your belonging as science educator. I sensed a tensionality between your fascination for science and abhorrence of science. I recollect you saying,

> Science is mind-boggling in its range. I have been thrilled by the moon landing, the probes of space, the material and agricultural advances, but even more, I am chilled by the threats—lingering, shadowing, haunting these positive gains.

Portraying the experience of tension within you, you offered a delightfully concrete metaphor: "a walking filing cabinet," pointing to how we tend to inhabit the categories, each housed in its own file. The one file that caught my fancy was the file under *R* (you labelled it "READ THIS AGAIN. THIS IS HOPEFUL."), the file which, you said, allows you to turn your face "outward from the inheritance."

I like what you said so much that I opened a file in my own filing cabinet in my study. And I used your label. I see in this gesture a coming into being of a tension at the interface between this file and all the others. And I like it.

In this connection, I recall a conversation with you during the AERA session on the meaning of "the same and the different." In the conversation, we were concerned about the way we pay homage to the primary of sameness and the way in which we either grant secondness to difference or become indifferent to difference. Do you remember that conversation? It went something like this:

Ted: We who are "identity"-oriented seem to be "sameness"-oriented, and we tend to depreciate the notion of "difference." Have you thoughts about how the two might be better understood?

Mary: Let's admit categorizing is a way of handling the world. We have to when we are given to prediction and control and organization of everything as we organize things in our filing cabinets. In that process, we lose or forget "differences." I'm opposed to the idea of final synthesis. I want to march forward in differences with bridges here and there..."

As I see it now, this little conversation of ours reflects a major theme in the ongoing modernism/postmodernism debate. I see in you a streak of postmodernism, questioning the metaphysical world that yields a synthetic totality of categories, a veritable fitting-together of your files into a single filing cabinet. Personally, I like this streak of yours.

Allow me a thought that flows from rereading the text of your last paper, "Knowing and Saying: Metaphors and Fragments." You offered us a choice metaphor: conversation as turnings. I like that. For with it, I can understand your and your colleagues' four years of conversations as a series of hermeneutic turnings: some short, others wide; some gentle, others deep.

One more thought. In rereading your three papers that came into being these four years, I tried to be sensitive to the language of each paper. Most notable as I reread them is the transformation in your languaging. It seems that the language of your first paper, "What Are We Interpreting? The Data Problem," is very apropos in the academic setting of the AERA conferences. This is in keeping with your concern with how fidelity to the "external requirements" (your words) of the AERA yields prosaicness resulting in a distanced reportage shorn of "the holy and the mystery that are found in journals," as one of your colleagues mentioned back in 1984. I compare it to the language of the last paper, "Knowing and Saying: Metaphors and Fragments." Do you recall my comment at the AERA session, when I entered into conversation with you following your presentation? I said:

> In reading your paper and now listening to you, I became animatedly poetic—and your sayings carried me to new seeings as you yourself seem to be in play in the words, at times frolicking in the words. I enjoyed being in your words.

Even now I am drawn into the themed texture of this paper:

> In the theme *knowing before saying,* you said that "metaphoric insight shows that one is always on the verge of things... " You have a yen for edges. Can you say more about the nature of the place where metaphors dwell?
>
> In the theme *saying before knowing, searching for metaphors in conversation,* you said, "Conversation, the turning, becomes a metaphor for unity, a temporary healing of the world's fragmentation." I find "conversation as healing" a refreshing notion. I would like to hear more.
>
> In the theme *saying with knowing through writing,* you said, "Writing... lacking gesture, needs [to] be more graceful, tentacled, reaching out, seeking to attract another's mind." A seductive thought. Have you read Roland Barthes' *The Pleasure of the Text?* You will like his languaging, I'm sure.
>
> In the theme *saying with knowing to guide others and self,* you said... "conversations... guided by metaphor are less fragmented," and in interpreting "teaching," you guided us through "teacher as gardener," "teacher as transmitter," and "teacher as pilgrim." The last one suggests "teaching as pilgrimage." I like it. I sense a sacredness.
>
> In the theme *revisiting metaphor previously held,* you referred to your twofolded understanding of "inheritance," a twofoldedness that unfolded itself over the four years in and through conversation. I am buoyed by your transformation from inheritance within the metaphor of "filing cabinets" to that within the metaphor of "a web of understanding." I see in this transformation a true turning.

I, on my own, have been wrestling with the arboreal metaphor (tree/roots metaphor), within whose inheritance I know I am caught. I like your metaphor of "web of understanding." I have been to my "READ THIS AGAIN. THIS IS HOPEFUL" file, and I've been reading about a web-like metaphor that Gilles Deleuze and Felix Guattari speak of in *A Thousand Plateaus.* It is the metaphor of rhizomes—a subterranean bed of tubers interconnected in ways different from "the roots-trunk-branches" nexus dominant in our thinking. Voices from beyond the edge? What do you think?

Is the time for another turning nigh? I await impatiently for renewed conversations with you. When is your next visit to the far northwest?

References

Barthes, R. (1975). *The pleasure of the text.* NY: Hill & Wang.

Deleuze, G. and F. Guattari. (1987). *A thousand plateaus.* Minneapolis: University of Minnesota Press.

Jessie's Voice

Being in community was a prominent feature of my life as I was the youngest member of my immediate family of four adults and a sister, and this unit was surrounded by many relatives in the area... So there were always aunts, uncles, cousins, and even faux relatives to enjoy and to care for. Church, school groups, and scouting offered broader but still rather intense opportunities for being with others. As I moved into adolescence I became engrossed with matters of the biological and physical sciences, an interest which at that time in my life was strong enough to give guidance to my college plans. I thought I wanted to be a laboratory technician, but I also wanted a degree, so I decided on a program that would accomplish both. However, I soon learned via field trips to labs that I wanted more interaction with people than that profession promised, and so I prepared to be a teacher.

As I reflect on my life journey in the papers in this text, I recall Barry Lopez' essay on landscape and narrative in which he speaks of two landscapes—"one outside the self, the other within" (1988). In story Lopez sees the two landscapes coming together in a harmony that is engendered by an intimate context. For me, telling the story of my journey has been an experience in bringing together my inner and outer landscapes, and this experience has been made possible by the intimacy of our group which patiently supported my efforts. Although persons in and outside of our group have figured prominently in my integrating inner and outer landscapes, there always emerges a thread that enables me to live more vividly with expression. That thread is music. For me music moves, excites, heals, and transcends.

Music prompts many pictures on my journey—pictures of a family life drawn together in many ways. "Daddy, please play the piano and sing" was a frequent request I made of my father. And my older cousins, one of whom always seemed to be living with us, would ask Uncle Ariel to sing—sing for them in the living room, sing for their weddings, and sing for the church talent supper. When company gathered and we were asked to play the piano, in spite of our protestations that the company never "listened to our pieces," we were reminded that we should be proud of our talents and share them. Also vividly portrayed in the pictures in my past is sitting on the edge of my seat at the Community Concert Series, straining to see Byron Janis at the keyboard or to hear Rise Stevens sing. How special to be a child among the adults at these concerts which usually lasted until 11:00 p.m. on a school night!

In grade school I sang with my classmates in holiday performances, but in high school I finally achieved my long-desired goal—full membership in the Modern Choir! We opened every concert with Fred Waring's arrangement of Say It with Music, and with that sound I soared! It was also during this time in my life that I directed the children's choir at church and played the organ, first as a substitute, then as a regular. Attending my father's former church for Welsh songfests was a special time to experience the fervor and talents of a group of singers who reveled in their musical heritage.

And today I am a voice student who, upon entering the fine arts building for my lesson, is transported into another world. The sounds of vocalizing and of the piano that squeeze through the cracks at the bottom of the studio doors announce to me that I am on a self-selected detour in my daily professional journey on campus. However, as soon as my lesson begins, the detour becomes part of the journey that started many years ago—a journey in which I have embraced music in a variety of ways. Although music is more a way of being for me than a vocation, it does help me be with my students and see them and myself as we work and play together. I try to listen to the many voices of my students in solo, in duets, in quartets, or other groupings. What do they and I hear in these different patterns or combinations? When do my students and I experience harmony, dissonance? How do I deal with dissonance? In music I generally prefer harmonies that resolve and, where possible, select to listen to or sing that kind of music. But avoiding dissonance is not always a choice in the classroom. What of movement and tempo? One of our group laughingly suggests that I usually select allegretto for my tempo. Perhaps I might select a detour in which adagio is the tempo.

Whatever characterizes the next detour I take or the next pictures I find within, I feel certain that music will continue to be an accompaniment that helps bring together the internal (self) and external (others) aspects of my life.

Reference

Lopez, B. (1988). Crossing open ground. *New York: Charles Scribner's Sons.*

Perceiving Self in Text

In this first piece, I share my efforts to enter the texts we created in our initial meetings as a group in teaching together. In this process, I endeavored to listen with care to the meanings that emerged and to be cognizant of the process I employed in uncovering meanings expressed in the first line of my text's melody.

Introduction

The centrality of the person in life processes is a theme that has guided my teaching, writing, and researching. Specific manifestations of this theme include inquiry into how one perceives self as teacher, as researcher, and as student. Therefore, even though I read our group's texts without consciously looking for indications of perceptions of self, the theme or form emerged and demanded of me that I examine it anew, but this time in the context of an inquiry group experience. I sought to understand perceptions of self as revealed in the personal texts or language of seven women who initially met to share research interests. What does the experience of being a member of this discussion group mean to the participants? What do the texts we created suggest about our perceptions of self as researchers, teachers, and members of an inquiry group?

In trying to answer these questions, I sought to understand our individual selves and our group selves as presented in the texts we created during our time together. I am part of the text and part of the context in which the texts were created; so my attempt to understand was also an attempt to increase my self-understanding. These efforts to understand were aided by Smith's explanation of *verstehen* from the interpretive-idealist perspective in which *verstehen* is viewed as "an attempt to achieve a sense of meaning that others give to their own situation through an interpretive understanding of their language, art, gesture, and politics (1983, 12). At the first level of this process, I tried to discover the *what* or the immediate apprehension of the human action which in this case is our expression of views of self. At the second level, I attempted to understand the *why* or the meaning assigned to the action. At this level, I tried to discover the meanings in my description of our perceptions and why we might have expressed these perceptions within the group context.

Views of Self: The Immediate Apprehension

As I read and reread our personal texts, I attempted to focus on more explicit statements of self, but some of my descriptions came about by teasing out implicit meanings—those perceptions of self that seem to be implied. In addition, even though I included many summary statements and have not quoted extensively, I tried to remain true to the language of the situation.

In our earlier texts in which we gave reasons for coming to the group, we described an interaction in our professional lives, discussed what the group interactions meant to us, and suggested our views of self as teacher, colleague, and researcher. There were the comfortable, almost warm perceptions of self expressed in phrases such as being cared for, wanting to be part of the group, enjoying the process of collaborating, seeing self as one of a group of kindred souls, getting excited about ideas, and playing with new concepts. In this spirit Louise offered, "The group reinforces my own need to become only what I can become. The outside world tries to cast me in a mold."

Then there were statements about self that suggested movement, hoped-for change, understandings, and concerns about the self in the group. Related to the latter, Francine described her holding enthusiasm for pursuing a hermeneutic phenomenological orientation with the group "somewhat in check as I sensed that maybe I was being too selfish and controlling of the group's direction." One of us spoke of a need for a sense of integration in life, and others saw self as becoming part of a true dialog after some initial reserve and as enjoying the challenge of being open to critical examination of issues from many perspectives. The feeling of *being,* of *becoming* was expressed by several persons when describing themselves as members of the group. Accompanying this feeling of being in process was the need to catch up, to learn which fences one was straddling, and to move one to shed the old, not by just adding the new, but somehow to achieve a new being that takes the best of the old and incorporates, refines, extends it in the new.

A subtheme or form which literally jumped out is the tension we experience as we live in two worlds. Francine "felt especially alone" in a context that did not share her perspective on interpretive inquiry. Contradictions, loneliness, selling one's soul (if only for a while) are words and phrases we used to describe our feelings about self as we sought to know who we are and what we are in the different worlds we inhabit. The aloneness of being in an institutional setting that drowns out our cry to be heard—to offer alternatives was one of my views of self as professor. And the loneliness of living with an ambivalent self or a self that is unknown to us, although to some degree more unknown in some settings than in others, was also part of our text. Still another member of the group spoke of many worlds within self that, at least for that person, needed to be integrated.

And finally, what one might view as opposite to warm, comfortable feelings are the cries of doubting self, not knowing self, and distress at seeing self in these ways. Diane confessed to still not feeling a member of the group, still wondering if we first should be dealing with the *questions* we need to be asking, not a method of inquiring. And another of us spoke of seeing self as less enthusiastic, less a contributor, and more self-conscious than when the group began. This stream or continuum of view of self that emerged in our earlier writings presents a multifaceted picture of seven women who are individuals but who also hold much in common when viewing self.

In the latest text we created, we wrote of the impact that the group has had on us. In studying these texts I found threads similar to ones in the earlier texts, and I found different ones. Also, since this later text focused more specifically on self, it probably contained more direct and fewer implied views of self. One participant spoke about her feelings of inadequacy in the process, but at the same time said that our work together had reinforced and encouraged her innate propensities. Our discussions helped Mary come to a "clearer understanding of dialectic." She goes on to say, "This has been supportive of my work in that it convinces me that I can interpret student dialog positively and in a way that can be shared with them—I don't have to reduce their thoughts to a little heap." Jana now sees "a new understanding of why [she] has so much anger, and why [she] has felt for a year that [her] work of research on the dialog journals wasn't going anywhere." Jana now sees herself as in transition, but also willing to speak with a more authentic voice.

Some texts spoke of hoped-for change that has not occurred. There was still some sense of self as unhappy, incomplete, and even less enthusiastic as a participant in the group. In another vein Diane questions, "Do I even stand a chance if I fail to fit the mold? Can I prostitute my soul for just a little while? I'll buy it back when I'm firmly entrenched in a career." But later she spoke of the group as having made her care again about the very important issues ... that seeking knowledge is inextricably woven into the search for self.

Yes, the puzzlement, ambiguity, and dissatisfaction were still evident in the later texts, but there were also statements of learnings about self in new ways, of a reinforcing of perceived self, and of some resolution that contributed to a heightened sense of self as worthy and whole.

Perceptions of Self: Meanings

As I examine the text I created in describing my immediate apprehension of how we perceived ourselves, I see my attempts to capture as vividly as possible how we viewed ourselves as individuals in the early and later parts of our experience as a group. At both times, I sense a range of perceptions of self, but in some areas the range has narrowed, perhaps even blurred in that some conflicts appear to have been resolved, and at times new, challenging, and pleasing perceptions have emerged. For some of us the view of self as at odds with the workplace or with the research community seems to have softened. Perhaps the opportunity to share openly feelings of hurt, rejection, and loneliness with people we trust and prize has made us feel more confident, more a part of a group that cares. Perhaps this talking together has given us alternatives and the courage to be ourselves.

What also seems to unfold in my text is the depth of impact that inquiring together has had on the individual members. The deep cry of anguish, the exhilaration of being part of the group, and the piercing questions seem to suggest a moving beyond surface or polite interactions: questions about "selling self" in the marketplace of ideas; questions about the nature of one's interactions with the group and whether they are helpful; questions about how real one's perceptions are of others and how one is seen by others; and finally, questions of how one can engage in interpretive inquiry with others and not hurt them in the process. The deep concern for the other in this process seems to accompany the questions and concerns about self. Why a seeming depth of response? Perhaps the lack of an externally imposed structure on our interactions; perhaps the socialness of our gatherings; perhaps the trust in and respect for each other that developed as we progressed.

Another meaning that seems to unfold in my text is that, as a group, we see ourselves as *being* and that we are accepted, liked, cajoled, teased because of what we *are* and not because of what we do. Products, counting accomplishments, although perhaps discussed as other-world criteria and concerns, do not seem to be part of our true dialog. Although each of us is unique in our approach to life, we have experienced a we-ness that has provided a context for trying to make sense out of individual worlds. We were not accountable to each other as persons except in the sense that we wished to be. There were no external rewards awaiting us unless one perceives "being accepted" on the American Educational Research Association program as a reward. It would be interesting to see which direction(s) the group would have taken had we not committed ourselves to the presentation.

As I ponder what new understandings, reforms, and extensions might grow out of my search for dialogical meaning in the text, the following emerges: Our group seems to be a community that seeks and gives to each other enlivenment, support, and courage. How might this be sustained? Should it be sustained? How do we know if and in what ways we can change our community? What would happen to each of us if we were to continue to study our community?

Another area of questioning which could lead to understanding relates to the possibilities for our being in community outside our group—building a community where the safety, caring, and support are perhaps absent or not as evident. Has our experience together enabled us to contribute to building community in other settings? Would we be able to *be* in a group that is more interested in *doing* or in the *completed*? Are these necessarily either-or? What of the both-and view of life that I am trying to integrate into my own perceptions of self in the world and in my own teaching and research?

What characterizes our celebrations in our group? We rejoice in a new bold step one has taken. We rejoice in the opportunity to immerse ourselves in a manuscript already published or one that one of us is preparing for publication, and we rejoice in our being together. To what degree might these moments of celebration be experienced in other settings? Can new understandings be experienced as we move in and out of our group and in what ways do the understandings vary with the setting?

Implications for Practice

What might my participation in the group and my attempt to understand our personal texts mean for my daily interactions with students and colleagues? My commitment to the centrality of the person in curriculum development has been reinforced and strengthened through our group interactions, but many questions remain. How can we know how students perceive themselves? In which situations is it beneficial to teacher and to student to share perceptions of self? How can perceptions of self be shared in a nonthreatening and caring context? I have been using dialog journal-writing with my students to share ideas, concerns, and feelings about self. So far this procedure *appears* to encourage an open sharing of self, but I still have many questions about this practice.

From another perspective, shared perceptions of self can be viewed in terms of how they facilitate teachers' reflecting upon and examining the learning contexts they make available to students. In what ways do settings for learning contribute to, highlight, or discourage perceptions of self in positive or negative ways? How might teachers change contexts in attempts to help students see themselves in different ways—as competent, decisive, caring, wondering, contributing, and valued individuals?

As I reconsider our texts and my theme of perceiving self, questions about research also emerge. Could the open, honest discussions of self as researchers that occurred in our group become part of our research discussion with our colleagues? How much, when, and in which contexts? If we dare not yet reveal ourselves to that extent in our daily interactions with colleagues, perhaps we can with our students. Research courses can examine why individuals choose to explore some questions and not others, why certain assumptions are made, and why data are conceptualized in certain ways. The writings of researchers such as Ross Mooney and Kaoru Yamamoto, in which they have made public their search for finding self in the knowledge-generating processes, can be studied. To acknowledge the impact of self on our research, to talk about it, and to write about it can reveal to us and others our perceptions of self. To what end? Perhaps to a growing awareness of who we are, why it is important to know self and others, and how the self creates and is created by the research we do.

When I face myself as I have in this group and in this analysis of text, I am confronted with how I perceive myself, the knowledge I value, and how and to whom I wish to communicate these insights. As I confront myself in this manner I see anew how the practice of teaching and research I engage in is directly influenced by how I perceive myself and by what I have learned about self through our group interactions.

Reference

Smith, J. K. (1983). Quantitative versus qualitative research: An attempt to clarify the issue. *Educational Researcher, 12 (3),* 6–13.

Teaching as Journeying in Community

> *Self in community continues to be a persistent theme in the melody of my texts. In this line the metaphor of teaching as journeying predominates, and the process of trying to identify the question my text seems to be answering provides the accompaniment.*

Our group continues to meet and in so doing, as Diane expressed, "creates a quilt of fabric whose warp and woof are connectedness and meaning-making." As we gather around the table we share our questions, concerns, creations of text and food, and we offer support, encouragement, humor, and enlightenment. We are connected by our being which transcends, as Mary reminds us, the reality that each of us has a different inheritance. That we have carved our life studies from various stones enriches our connectedness and supports us in our commitment to relationships and to helping each make her individual journey.

Journey: Context for Reflecting

As I reflect on the relationships that have been engendered in our group, I see us in teaching with each other, and the knowledge that is generated and shared within the group is knowledge "that originates not in curiosity or control but in compassion, or love" (Palmer 1983, 8). The knower and known become one in this context we create, and our knowing "draws not only on our senses and our reason, but on our intuitions, our beliefs, our actions, our relationships..." (p. xii). It is within this context that I see us seeking out each other as teachers.

During the time I was experiencing this sense of teaching in our group, I was also coteaching a course on campus with Mary-Ellen Jacobs, a graduate student new to the field of teacher education. In this context I again found teaching to be a sharing of knowledge and a seeking out of each other. We planned face to face, in writing, and on the phone; we experienced various ways of becoming a team; and we reflected on our teaching formally after each class and more informally between planning periods. The metaphor of *Teaching as Journey* gradually emerged in our discourse as we planned for our tour, the stops, and the baggage we would need. We accepted and at times welcomed the ever-recurring detours, and we even spoke of ourselves as copilots on this journey. As I reflected on our coteaching experiences, I saw the genesis of this journey in earlier letters we exchanged about graduate school matters when we were advisee and advisor, and I noted that the humor and metaphoric expressions that laced our exchanges as coteachers were also present in our initial interactions. And as if, perhaps subconsciously, to continue this pattern, we identified written composition as a major focus in our undergraduate language arts methods course, and we invited our students to join us in studying that part of our journey.

As I continued to see myself as being in teaching with my coteacher and with our group, I was motivated to deeper reflection by the following questions:

What is it like for me to be in teaching in our group, and what was it like to be in teaching with another in a formal school context?

What does experiencing teaching in these two contexts teach me about myself as teacher and about the connections between two journeys that are both similar and different?

Which meanings transcend the immediate experiencing of the two journeys and open possible new vistas, new insights about self in a collaborative context?

In seeking responses to these questions, I learned that, for me, journey and tour are comfortable metaphors in which to reside. From the French *journée* and the Latin *dies* comes a view of journey as a daily course of the sun through the heavens, and from the Greek *ropvos* comes the word for a tool describing a circle which also implies one's turning in order to do something. Course, circle, and order evoke visions of the sun's movement through time and space—a movement which bespeaks the promise of change, of detours, of unexpected sights and experiences, but also the promise of the cycle recurring again and again. The stability and predictability of the life cycle that embrace change create a context of safety and freedom that invites us to enjoy the unanticipated in the shape of detours that can open new paths, new possibilities, and new dreams. To experience with others my turning and the changing hues and shades of light and shadows of the sun's journey through the heavens is an invitation for me to reflect on what it is like to journey with another—to be in dialog with myself and others about teaching.

In attempting to live in metaphor, to see myself as teacher from the inside out, I initially reflected in dialog with others in our group. Then upon leaving the group, I engaged in a type of monolog in which I continued the dialog internally, but with much difficulty as I missed the comfort of the group context which offered opportunities to converse and to translate my inner language of participant into the language of the spectator (Britton 1970). The opportunity to tell my story and to hear it aloud in the presence of another was absent in the solitude of my study. Also absent was the chance to listen with care to another's stories, different stories, but stories that could help me listen to my own and to learn more about how I might become more open to diversity, to see others' ways of viewing the world—ways that may not be part of my life narrative. For in Mary's words, we need opportunities to "get beyond our finite history."

What are the questions the group offers? What are the questions about my narrative of journeying in community that help me listen to my own story and try to identify the question my story asks? The group asks: How did my role change as I experienced teaching with another? Does collaborating expressed in coteaching encourage me to create different contexts and to see them in different ways? What have I learned about myself that is surprising? And, what characterizes the language in our context of journeying in community? As I struggle with answering and raising questions about my journey, I constantly seek and find nourishment and support in experiencing and recalling the group's dialog.

What Is It Like for Me to Journey in Dialog with Another?

To be in teaching as journeying in community is to be both alone and together. Although as a group, team, or pair we create by planning, guiding, and reflecting in community, our unique individuality shines through. My stitches in our group quilt bear the mark of my individuality, and they also contribute to the overall pattern. I find that knowing the sun will rise again—that there will always be another opportunity and that collaborating is a work of fashioning a tapestry that reflects a joint weaving—encourages me to question, to enrich, and not just to challenge.

And when I am home alone in my study basking in the quiet afterglow of the setting sun, I breathe shallowly at first, but with increasing depth, the breath of the day's experiencing. Carried on the air I breathe is my struggle with asking questions of the text I share with the group.

Also in the airstream are my thoughts about the leg of the tour my colleague and I traveled that day with our students. The reflective dialog we engaged in after class seemed to make sense; certain meanings appeared to emerge, but now alone in my home, the meanings take on a different hue and texture. What did I say? Is that what I meant to say? What was it like for my colleague or our group members to try to respond to my narrative, to offer new perspectives, to think about their own feelings and ideas within the context of the ones I shared? What was I asking of them in requesting that they listen to me rehearse my story? Did I listen? Why is it difficult for me to make the transition from dialog to monolog? Could my preference for dialog be part of the reason for my rather consistently seeking collaborators?

In a larger sense, I think about what my students experience when they leave the class context. Do they struggle with trying to incorporate group-generated meanings into their personal meanings? Do I ever inquire into this possible struggle in a manner that enriches and not just challenges? I also wonder about grading papers in which I evaluate responses related to meanings that *I* think we created. Could this process be an example of asking or perhaps, if I'm honest, requiring students to codify meanings generated in one context and then move them to another expecting they will have meaning in the latter context?

On tour we constantly change contexts. What is it like? What adaptations, perspectives can help us live fully in each context? In pondering this question I return to the notions of day, circle, and turning, and I am reminded of *Anno's Journey* in which he writes: "I wandered from town to town, from country to country, and sometimes my journey was hard, but it is just such times the reward comes" (1982, unpaginated). Anno's world was anchored in a deep-rooted sense of culture and an appreciation of nature. My world of teaching as journeying in community is anchored in the belief that when one tours with another, the journey is enriched for all.

In what ways has language shaped my journeying in community? Journey, tour, community, connecting, quilting are predominant metaphors that remind, in that they bring to mind and "encourage us to discover relationships and how they might be articulated. Metaphors are thus heuristic in function" (Berthoff 1981, 7). My teammate and I were on tour; we were copilots; and we experienced detours which I attempted to view as possibility and not hindrance. Yes, metaphor directed our thinking, our language, and our actions.

Another aspect of the language context that causes me to think deeply about teaching is how we use language to describe what we are and do in teaching. My copilot used current labels to describe teaching procedures and processes she had recently learned. Concept attainment was one label she used when describing a learning activity designed to make it possible for students to engage in inductive thinking. I ask myself: New labels for old vessels? Not necessarily, but hearing the current labels helped me reflect on what I do intuitively after many years of teaching. The injection of new labels, new ways of naming the world, became a focus for dialog. In this dialog we seemed to see our initial more separate roles of teacher and student begin to give way to our becoming collaborators. Trying on new labels and reflecting on how I name my world raises questions about the function of labeling and naming in my students' learning to become teachers. What of the power of naming our world? When do we feel it helpful or necessary to name our world? Mary hunches that when we see ourselves as being the world, we have no need to try to name it.

Pondering teaching as journey, tour, and community which includes dialog with self and others has given me an opportunity to take a look from the inside out at being in teaching in our group and with another as coteacher. I think I now have some notion of the question my narrative continues to seek to answer: What is it like to see again two teaching experiences through the metaphor of teaching as journeying in community?

References

Anno, M. (1978). *Anno's journey.* New York: Philomel Books.

Berthoff, A. (1981). *The making of meaning: Metaphors, models, and maxims for writing teachers.* Montclair, NJ: Boynton/Cook.

Britton, J. (1970). *Language and learning.* Coral Gables, FL: University of Miami Press.

Palmer, P. (1983). *To know as we are known: A spirituality of education.* San Francisco: Harper & Row.

Contemplating Detour

Here is yet another variation on the theme of self in community. In this line of the melody, exploring detour as context for doing heartwork on the pictures within me offers images that open new vistas for viewing detour as making dwelling possible. The accompaniment of process made explicit in the last two papers is piano, and the melody sings!

Early in our being together as a group, I reflected on perceptions of self in the curriculum as I sought to understand myself and the other members of the group as revealed in the texts we created. The two questions that guided my search and seemed to underlie our texts were: What does the experience of being a member of this group mean to the participants, and what do the texts we have created suggest about our perceptions of self as researchers, teachers, and members of an inquiry group? My reading and rereading of our texts revealed that we anguished together about our being in our different worlds; we enjoyed and appreciated each other for what we as individuals were and not what we had done; we valued our uniqueness in community; and we celebrated! We celebrated new steps, new insights, new understandings, but mostly we seemed to celebrate being together.

In my second paper, "Teaching: Journeying in Community," I reflected on my experience of coteaching an undergraduate class and on being in teaching with our group. Again, the desire to know self emerged in the question my text seemed to be asking: What is it like to experience teaching in community? In this text I focused on the other and on my attempt to know self by reflecting on my dialog with self and significant others. At times when dialoging about our teaching, my team-mate and I were copilots on tour experiencing many detours.

Initially, when I reread the journeying in community paper, detour did not emerge as a major theme. However, as I read it again and again and reviewed the typescript of the dialog Ted and I engaged in during the presentation of that paper, detour became more prominent. It became clear to me that my copilot's offering me a new meaning for detour—detour as possibility, not hindrance—was a significant gift that I wanted to receive and try to make mine. In addition, Ted's comments on detour as a "very important element," his question "how do you understand detour?" and his wondering why a detour is necessary to get to go home provided additional motivation to delve more deeply into my experiencing detour—to contemplate detour. And so was born the idea for this paper.

Exploring the meaning that experiencing detour had for me was heightened by my meditating on the following by Rainer Maria Rilke:

> Work of sight is done
> Now do heart work
> On the pictures within you. (Rainer Maria Rilke, *Turning*)

A torrent of questions flooded my mind! What is sight work in my life? What are the pictures within me? In which ways might they color the pictures I create of others? How do others perceive the fruits of my heart work? What might the metaphor of *Curriculum as Detour* mean to students and teachers? In pondering these questions, I found myself trying to make connections between detour and context—the latter one of my persistent life interests. Might detour be perceived as context for heart work?

Detour: Context For Heart Work

When I first presented a sketch of my thoughts on detour to our group, Diane suggested that reflecting on the images or pictures I create could be interpreted as viewing "pictures as a detour in this process of making meaning through language." I liked this idea, for it gave me the courage I needed to pursue detour as one path to knowing more about self. In thinking about detour as context for heart work, I considered many meanings of hearts, but *central and innermost* seemed most appropriate to heart work or the creating of pictures within—pictures that quietly (wordlessly) portray our innermost thoughts, feelings, and perceptions in hues and lines which illumine possibilities of movement and connections.

Richard Kearney's conversation with Paul Ricoeur about Ricoeur's contributions to contemporary thinking provided additional support for viewing detour as context for heart work. For in the conversation, Ricoeur speaks of his commitment to apprehending the meaning of existence through language mediations which can be perceived as detours (Kearney 1984, 22). This seeking meaning, turning to oneself, peeling back the layers to reach the essence of being or the core of self could flourish in a certain sense of time and space encompassed in the notion of detour as a turning away from the most direct or shortest route. As one leaves the main road to take a detour of one's own or another's choosing, clock time can give way to *kairos* or the experiencing of unmeasured time, and metered space steps aside for uncharted openness. We can be, we can be experiencing, we can inhale the beauty before us without counting miles and minutes.

This turning *away from,* which can also nurture a *turning to* self, opens to the traveler opportunities to contemplate, to ponder possibilities the detour unfolds. Inherent in the idea of contemplating offered by my teammate is *templum,* or an open space marked by auguries which signal opportunities for observations and interpretations. In such time spaces we can nourish a sensitivity which, like Vermeer's work, guides people in "looking not for the obviously special event, but instead for extraordinary grace in simple household moments" (Polster 1987, 9). On recent detours I have experienced this new awakening to the simple heretofore unnoticed and unappreciated aspects of life. Details on a card, the personal modification or embellishment of an already meaningful picture, the significance of a grocery bag used to express a feeling of caring, and the quiet facial changes of an elderly patient when company comes—a gentle, weak ray of hope. This opening up of possibilities, this seeing what *can be* moves us beyond the fate of Meursault in Camus' *The Stranger* where everything is seen as is—no possibilities.

We can experience detour positively as just proposed, but we can also perceive it somewhat negatively—as a shattering of desired wholeness. In this latter sense of detour, road blocks and disarray loom large prompting caution and sometimes even halting action. What happens when I slow down? Dare I move into *kairos*? How difficult is it to place behind me the straight of the predetermined, to listen to my inner self when I cannot see the end of the journey? What does it take for me to be open to a different light, and if I can be open to it what might it mean for me to carry that light with me when I return? Viewing detour as barrier and disjunction might cause one to feel out of control, but experiencing detour as a turning inward that reveals possibilities can give a new kind of control which frees and which transforms the unplanned into wonders. Even though at times experiencing detour might mean living with discontinuity and discord, there are still the options of allowing and accepting the serendipitous, of making connections though unplanned, and of seizing opportunities to examine the meaning of the discordant in our lives.

Curriculum Connections

Heart work can become the work of students when curriculum is viewed as detour in which we create contexts that invite persons to invent and to initiate in visual as well as verbal images. Students can be invited to view their pictures or images as windows which open or close at the artist's wish, which let light in and send light forth, and which can be framed with the students' chosen boundaries. We can also explore with students what they include and what they exclude in their pictures. Perceiving self as initiator and as creator is an aspect of context in which heart work can flourish, one which is vital to composing visually, orally, or in writing.

Viewing curriculum as detour can also have implications for how persons in schools journey together. How do we respond to detours that we choose and those that are imposed on us? What are the consequences of our not taking the detour outlined by others? How might we see detour predetermined, not chosen, as challenge, not barrier? What is required of us to do heart work on a detour imposed upon us or one in which we constitute the minority voice? In essence, what characterizes decision-making in a context in which we have little or no input? How do teachers respond to last-minute schedule changes. What does it take to encourage heart work in this context?

Another aspect of detour that we experience in curriculum is the quality of being part of a larger whole. What happens when we take time to dwell in a part of the whole? Are there differences when the part is chosen or predetermined? How might we weave this experiencing of the part into the fabric of the larger journey? In which ways might we do this alone and in community? A student offers that a class discussion brings to mind a favorite poem. What might it mean for this student or the class to dwell on this part of the whole? In which ways might this detour encourage heart work? How is the ensuing journey changed as a result of carefully considering this portion of the larger context?

I am reminded of a recent conversation with one of my advisees which began with her request for advice in course selection. We discussed possibilities for a bit, then I encouraged the student to tell me something about herself since that was our first meeting. She related the story of her disappointment in not getting her preferred instructor in one of her classes, but she assured me with her words and a look of resolve that she was used to "making do" in life and proceeded to tell me what could be a sad life story except for her strength in dealing with life contingencies. After traveling this detour with her, I wondered what she would bring to the teaching profession—not varied or deep cultural experiences in the more traditional sense, not the appearance that some school administrators seek, but a commitment to persons, a strength of struggle, and a faith in her ability to accomplish what she sets out to do. I do not know what she took from that detour, but I know that my experiencing that detour with her has made me again acknowledge the importance of noticing the parts which constitute the whole of our students' lives.

Detour can also have implications for planning. What opportunities for planning in different contexts can we offer students? How do we plan when there is a change in routine, when time is not so bounded by the clock, when space is open, but when there are still markers to guide our contemplating? When viewed as possibility, detour has the potential for creating a context in which we see opportunities for welcoming the sependipitous, for making connections, and for living with what at first might seem to lack continuity but which has potential for becoming part of the fabric of the larger journey.

Personal Reflections on Contemplating Detour

In what ways do I know myself anew as I contemplate detour and as I make these contemplations public? Dwelling in the concept of detour has encouraged my doing heart work as evidenced by my efforts to leave the dizzying daily race with time to visualize, read, think, and write. My image of detour is consistent—open, rolling hills carved by a meandering road bordered with patches of fields and clumps of verdant trees and bushes roofed with billowing white puff clouds. Is it possible that this pastoral scene reflects my desire, search for wholeness? Will this picture change my former view of detour as annoyance, interruption, and barrier? Perhaps the imaging alone will not effect the change, but the resolve to experience detour as invitation to see more deeply and openly and the telling of this experience accompanied by the pictures I create will help me change.

Narrative and heart work are a both-and in this perspective on detour. Narrative makes it possible for us to give order and coherence to life, and heart work enables us to open up to ourselves, to others, and to life possibilities in general. I like to think that telling this story about detour will help me make transitions and "lean into nextness" (Polster 1987, 42). It is also possible that, as Ricoeur proposes, telling my story enables me to "acquire an identity" (Kearney 1984, 21).

Polster's definition of metaphor as a guiding image which "consolidates much of a person's life into a single, representative picture" (1987, 91) affirms the notion of a *templum* for creating pictures out of our observations and interpretations. I have become keenly aware of the dangers of trying to push a metaphor too far, but I have also gained a new appreciation of the struggle to achieve a successful metaphor which "demonstrates that the maker of the metaphor has developed both a keen sensitivity to language and a strong awareness of the unity of all things" (Bartel 1983, 83).

Contemplating pictures as detour has revealed to me a multitude of possibilities—sharp colors and lines, soft hues gently shaped by muted boundaries, and rays reaching out to horizons unknown. Contemplation, the intense dwelling in space with markers I can choose or ignore in creating my pictures, takes on new meanings with each perceived and experienced detour. The experience has expanded what I know about myself and has given me another way for knowing—pictures. But there are still many pictures to be drawn:

> And out of what one sees and hears and out
> Of what one feels, who could have thought to make
> So many selves, so many sensuous worlds
> As if the air, the mid-day air, was swarming...
>
> (Wallace Stevens, *Esthétique du Mal*)

References

Bartel, R. (1983). *Metaphors and symbols: Forays into language.* Urbana, IL: National Council of Teachers of English.

Kearney, R. (1984). *Dialogues with contemporary continental thinkers: The phenomenological heritage.* Dover, NH: Manchester University Press.

Polster, E. (1987). *Every person's life is worth a novel.* New York: W. W. Norton.

Rilke, R. M. (1982). *Turning.* In S. S. Judson, The quiet eye: A way of looking at pictures. Chicago: Regnery Gateway, unpaginated.

Stevens, W. (1947). In *The Collected Poems of Wallace Stevens.* New York: Alfred A. Knopf, p. 115–125.

Ted in Conversation with Jessie

Rereading at one sitting three AERA "voices" of '84, '87 and '88, rekindled memories of our pre-conference conversation-by-mail and conversations during the symposia. Unfolded before me is your questioning over these years of what it means to be self, what the essence of teaching with others is, and what it is like to be on curricular journeys and detours. I have found in this unfolding a deepening of discourse with the flavor of poetic language that knows what it is to dwell humanly on earth.

For long you have been concerned about the way in which self has been understood narrowly as self-as-individual, and I know you have been exploring the self through "personhood," interpreted as being with others. I feel that the notion of "otherness," of which you are insistently mindful, allows us to be reminded of the fundamentally ethical way we must live as persons. Your thoughts remind me of how Emmanuel Levinas, who by accepting as you do the primacy of responsibility to others, makes his ethical phenomenology relevant to the task of undoing instrumentalism that tends to separate teaching acts from ethics and values.

As you unfolded yourself to a layered view of self-acknowledging the surface nature of "immediate apprehension" and the more grounded understanding of the "meaning of self," you allowed yourself to be gathered within the fold of a question which itself was twofolded. I recall you asking, "What does the experience of being a member of the study group mean to the participants, and what do the texts we have created suggest about perceptions of self as researchers, teachers, and members of an inquiry group?" This question indeed opened up for you new paths.

I remember at the 1987 AERA symposium when you were discussing your experiences of "Teaching: Journeying in Community," we discussed the possibility that the metaphor of "detour in a journey" might reveal a dimension of teaching often concealed. And I remember

vividly the time you exclaimed, "I worked through detour!!!" waving
to us the 1988 paper you titled, "Detour: Context for Heart Work."

All of us can recall detours we have taken in our lives. Hence, we
can in some respects relate with you concretely. But I doubt if many of
us have been thoughtful about the experience of detour as you have
been. You suggested to us that we reflect upon themes of detour, a few
of which you identified as "the shattering of wholeness," "opening to a
different light," "detouring as a turning that reveals possibilities of
transforming the unplanned into wonders." In connection with this,
what you wrote still remains cogently vibrant:

> Even though at times experiencing detour might mean living with
> discontinuity and discord, there is still the other option of allowing
> and accepting the serendipitous, of making connections though un-
> planned, and seizing opportunities to examine the meaning of the
> discordant in our lives.

You reached out for more. I liked your notion of "detour as a context for heart work"—kind of the heart work that allows *kairos,* the
experiencing of unmeasured time; the kind of heart work that allows a
seeing beyond the obvious to the extraordinary grace in simple household events; the kind of heart work that, even when one experiences a
shattering of wholeness, there is in the shattering the possibilities of
openness to a different light.

In light of the understandings you presented to us, I as curriculum
worker am tempted to plan for detours. I know you will likely slap my
hand for even saying that, for a detour planned is not detour. But kid-
ding aside, I wish to remember the question you surfaced in our last
conversation: "What is required of us to do heart work on a detour in
which we constitute the minority voice?"

Might you have an answer to this question? It would be for me a
pleasure indeed if you can allow this question to be the source of our
coming together in a renewed conversation.

Diane's Voice

In one of the papers to follow, I share my trepidation over committing words to text. "How will I be known?" I ask. Here I am given freedom to respond beyond the scope of convention, and yet I am hesitant to say more than just what might appear in the back of any book: "As an undergraduate I majored in sociology and psychology. My graduate emphasis was upon life-span human development with a special focus on aging and the aged, research, and statistics." This background has served me well: "I've taught courses related to development over the course of life as well as research methods in education. In the latter course I was responsible for the sections on quantitative methods. I am currently teaching courses in educational psychology and human learning and cognition."

Clearly, I have been interested in the processes underlying persons developing. Furthermore, I am well grounded in the positivistic tradition.

How then did I enter a group such as this, write for a book with this thrust? I spoke to this in one of my earliest papers for this group. "Research. Research. The word is provocative." The group would offer me an opportunity to explore questions of interest to me, with persons I believed shared my concerns.

I was not expecting what was to follow. I was prepared to share my research, to critique and lend support to others, to be critiqued and to receive support.

I recall a group meeting at Francine's. Jana asked us to identify a book that had been important to us as children, a book that we would label our favorite. We were also to describe our favorite character in the book and to talk about our choice. What did this have to do with

*research or with our professional concerns? I was the
first Jana called upon to respond. Hesitantly I stated,
"Louisa May Alcott's* Little Women. *Jo was by far my favorite. I read and reread that book. I loved that book. It
was a book about family, about caring, about growing,
about being. It was a book about finding and creating
meaning within loving relationships." I still treasure that
book and I still identify with the struggles Jo and her
sisters faced as they tried to understand and give shape
to their lives. Aha. The very things that made that book
so meaningful, so alive, to me as a child were themes
still important to me as an adult. But were they present
when I look to my teaching and research?*

*I had been purposefully taught to keep myself hidden
and apart from my research. I had been advised to wear
a mask of anonymity when I taught. I felt free to shed
the masks within the group but was finding myself quite
uncomfortable with this Janis-type existence.*

*I had replied hesitantly. How very typical of me. Even
within the comfort of the group I am often quiet, slow
to respond, and seldom eager to make known my inner
self. With each step forward there is forever a backward
glance. I do not write of the changes within in terms of
a turning or a detour. I speak of a leap. I do not walk
deliberately, slowly, looking forward. I hold my breath,
crossing boundaries while in flight, looking backwards.
I know that what was behind me will never appear as it
had before. And when I look forward I recognize that I
will never be quite the same either.*

*I enter every important decision this same way. Like
Jacob with the angel, each transforming event in my life
is preceded with deliberation, a struggle, and a leap.
There is oftentimes a change in name identifying the
change(s) in me, for to change a name is to change reality. Changes in my name signaled major transitions in
being and in consciousness. Diane Thompson became
Diane Lee. Three years later Diane also became Mom.*

*And when the student became a teacher, I became known
as Dr. Lee.*

*Looking back I see that it has always been in connec-
tion with others that I am transformed. Each time I take
flight, I soar with the spirit of others in my heart.*

*This chapter is about another transforming associa-
tion. It is about my being within a community of professional women, scholars and researchers, and my
attempt toward authentic participation.*

*With the title "assistant professor" came the realiza-
tion that I was indeed a member of the professional
ranks. I quickly came to question the full meaning of
being a professional. What did it mean to be a professional beyond receiving a paycheck, a title, and an office? What voices would define me as a professional?
Would I be able to integrate the many voices that give
shape to my life, or would I stand outside the situation,
safely hidden behind the technocratic tradition? What
was it about Jo that had made her such a special
teacher? It was not just her level of expertise, but rather
her ability, her willingness to care, to be concerned, and
thus to be fully engaged as a mother, a spouse, a teacher,
a woman, a person.*

*I, too, want to "be" in the truest, fullest sense of be-
ing. I am a child brought into this world in the midst of
a close, loving family. I am a wife, a partner in a loving
relationship. I am a mother of three sons whom I laughingly refer to as the bane of my existence and the light
of my life. I am a sister, an aunt, a friend, a teacher, a
researcher, a home-maker, and an active member of a
religious community. I have lived and worked all my
life within a forty-mile radius and remain deeply connected to this area. I am a woman defined within relationships; relationships that I care about and, therefore,
that constitute me.*

To Be in a World of Wicked Problems

In a collection of essays titled "Holzwege," Heidegger speaks of woodpaths. Wood is the name for forest, and he is speaking of winding paths that end quite suddenly in impenetrable thickets:

> *Each goes it's peculiar way, but in the same forest. Often it seems as though one were identical to another. Yet it only seems so. (in Krell 1977, 34)*

Woodpaths take one through the forest, but the traveler is not in total control of the direction or the final destination. Rather, woodpaths force the traveler into unknown territory and may even force the traveler to retrace previous steps.

In this first paper, I write about my beginning journey with persons familiar with the forest. They have chosen not to cut down trees or to bulldoze their way through. They have not chosen a final destination. They have selected a woodpath. I agree to the journey and begin to see the forest as I never had before.

Direct, linear paths are not ours. I express dissatisfaction with the old ways yet remain fearful of the unpredictable, uncontrollable, unreliable path I now face. I must commit my unmapped journey to faith. First, to faith in my fellow travelers and secondly to faith in myself. Embedded in care I find the source of my strength is in connection with others. Mastery, control, and a single source of knowledge are not as important as before. Hunches, vague perceptions, queasy feelings, and connections are guiding me through. I am still so frightened of the journey that I commit my recollections to spirit. I release my voice through my fingertips. Only later do I realize the significance of the boundaries I've crossed. But early on I realized I could only have crossed them in communion with others.

As is often the case, I left our group meeting with an assignment: to write about a particular experience that held special significance for me and to generate questions that would help me to understand how I determined that significance. I read some of my earlier entries and realized that, although the issues were still pertinent, some of the passion had dissipated. I was confronted by my old nemesis, however. Questions popped around in my head and I sat for a long, long time trying to determine which one deserved priority. In trying to decide, I realized once again how important context is in the process of decision. Do I choose a question that has meaning for our group? Do I choose a question that would feel most comfortable as a paper to be presented at AERA? Do I choose a question that has leading-on power for me— perhaps for me alone? I decided to sit at the keyboard as though some mystical force would enter my fingers, allowing me to escape decision. Truth and being. Truth and method. Truths. Methods. Ways of being. The words appeared, just appeared.

I had been discussing methods of evaluation with members of one of my graduate classes. They were hailing multiple choice as the most fair testing method:

"It's objective."
"The answer is either right or wrong. How well the teacher likes or dislikes you never enters into the picture at all."
"It's easy to grade. A computer can do it. Students won't be angry at you. You only keep score."

I did not hide my displeasure. "But," say I feeling somewhat betrayed, "knowledge is not always linear. Multiple choice exams can't be written to measure synthesis. (Can they?) What about the merit of debate? Of reasoning when it is evident that there is no one simple answer? And isn't education necessarily subjective? Persons relating to persons, together creating knowledge? Remember our discussion about..."

They could remember our discussion, but they were not yet prepared to translate the pedagogic experience into their own lived experience. I was disheartened. I had wanted them to accept my position. I had preached, but I had failed to take their perspective. I had ignored my own advice: "In teaching you begin with the persons in your class. Know them; know yourself. Know yourselves together. Then you can make wise curricular decisions."

This pattering about helped me to recall something I had read for a class I had taken with Jessie and Louise. Dewey used the term *mind* as a verb. He wrote about teachers acting mindfully, that is, in an active mode of paying heed, of caring, of futuring. For Dewey, to function mindfully meant to be able to support a great diversity of meanings, and those meanings would compose a background against which new learning experiences could be projected. The realm of meanings includes moral meanings, poetic meanings, and the kinds of meanings persons begin to engage when they work together to solve problems, to alter in some fashion the order of things (1958, 411). It seemed evident to me that mindful teachers would have to be subjective. Yet, as suggested by my students, it also seemed that teachers would have to be somewhat removed. Van Manen (1986) captured the essence of this dialectic. He wrote that teachers must know and make decisions for students with caring, thus they must be fully engaged, interacting with maximum subjectivity. On the other hand, he noted that teachers must be sensitive to students' total field of limits and possibilities, indicating a need for reserve and distancing. Van Manen and Dewey recognized the necessary inseparability of subjectivity and objectivity in the process of meaning-making. Teachers cannot be totally objective with students, nor can they be truly caring if they fail to actualize the epistimological and leading-on power aspects of caring that Louise describes (Berman 1968, 1977; Lee and Berman 1987). It seems to me that interpersonal relationships are guided by relative truths, by questioning what it means to experience the lifeworld of the classroom together. Aha!

Aha. The passion is returning and I can't type fast enough. My students were arguing for a method that presupposes a single truth. I was so dismayed because that mystical force that had taken over within me was intent on writing about problems that defy the notion of a single solution, a single truth. While ultimately one solution must be enacted at some point in time, problem definition and problem solving are processes that demand constant reconceptualization, for there are multiple solution paths. Thinking and problem definition are constrained by the contexts in which they occur and by individuals' interpersonal understandings. The theoretical distinctions highlighted by Churchman (1971) were taking on real meaning for me. Churchman wrote about "real life" and "wicked" problems in juxtaposition to puzzles. Puzzles result in a single correct solution, derived with the aid of a complete set of instructions or explicit rules. The problem space is closed, and parameters known. Wicked problems, on the other hand, are open to multiple solutions. Instructions alone provide insufficient information for problem solution. The problem space is broad, parameters unknown and in flux being responsive to context. More recently researchers are writing about these problems on the basis of a continuum of structuredness, from well- to ill-structured problems. Wood (1983) has done a marvelous job of articulating the structuredness of a problem. He notes that any problem solving situation involves a decision maker, the actions open to him or her, states of nature, possible outcomes, probabilities of states of nature given the decision maker's acts, and the utility of the solution to the individual. Well-structured problems entail relatively specific values for each of these parameters, while for ill-structured problems the value of one or more of the parameters is not known.

I wanted my students to realize that, to be authentic professionals, they would have to reject notions of fixed values, fixed goals, fixed objectives, fixed truths. I wanted them to be oriented to possibilities, to ways of being.

My being in the group has been rooted in conversation, inquiry, and questioning. Our group functions much like a prism. We each came with our own inheritance (taken from Mary's transcript), as Mary has so aptly labeled our pedagogical baggage. Through our thoughtful reflections, however, we have "funded a great diversity of meanings" and explored many of the "wicked problems" that are the everyday stuff of teaching, of being in the world of classrooms. Prior to coming to the group I was all too content to view but one or two sides of the prism. I was guilty of what Gadamer (1975) suggests occurs with technical rationales that fail to present their horizons—I was overvaluing what was nearest to me. Being in the group has nudged me to go beyond the confines of my inheritance. Our being together has created a situation wherein horizons have been expanded and mystery has been brought more fully into our presence (van Manen 1984). We are engaged in a curriculum of being. We seek vision that will bring "into nearness that which tends to be obscure, that which tends to evade the intelligibility of our natural attitude of everyday life" (van Manen undated manuscript 4). Our vision is founded upon a necessary tacit platform:

> Each situation represents a standpoint that limits the possibility of vision. Thus, the concept of a "horizon" is an essential part of each situation, and many thinkers have used the word to characterize the way in which thought is tied to a platform. It is this platform that allows us to see beyond what is nearest to us. Without such a platform we are limited to and overvalue what seems to have a sense of immediacy to us. (Macdonald and Purpel 1987, 184)

The group is my platform. It is a platform of words, of ideas about what is, and of visions of what ought to be (Walker in Macdonald and Purpel 1987, 185), what can be. Within our group I feel free to imagine, compelled to seek possibilities, and destined to journey toward new horizons. We are like travelers journeying together, as Francine suggests, comfortable with the uncertainty of our course and our destinations, reveling as we view from multiple perspectives the colors reflected in the prism we hold—our text.

To analyze the structures of our experience, we sought to uncover themes in our text. Many themes emerged from it, but one stood out to me: connectedness. Not surprisingly, we all found ourselves weaving patterns, albeit different in color and design, but with similar threads. Like the quilters of long ago, the warp and woof of our fabric was connectedness and meaning-making. Francine's trilogy (taken from her transcript)—person-to-person-to-object; we weave creating a tapestry, persons-to-persons together weaving a fabric. Our quilt brings warmth, comfort, caring. All the metaphors seem to create the patterns which flow from our fingertips. We "dish up" (Louise) as we engage in a "journey" (Francine) that is a "ministering of thoughtfulness" (van Manen undated manuscript 2). A team, truly "collaborative" (Jessie), creating a fabric that no one person will own. As we query about "what matters," the pattern the cloth will take emerges. There was no set design, no set of instructions. Questions. Many questions. Stitches were never ripped out, although occasionally resown or strengthened. Commitment. Fidelity (Noddings 1986). A vocation (Huebner 1987). Perhaps a calling, yes. We seek. We journey. We began at different places, found common junctures, journeyed together and when emersed in thoughtful reflection, journeyed alone. Our destinations? Perhaps not the same. Different "inheritances" (to some degree) add excitement to the weave and may be a factor in directing us to varied destinations, varied interpretations, multiple perspectives.

We've all chosen "wicked" problems; puzzles seldom enter our texts or our conversation. It is not by chance that we ponder over questions; we tend to reject absolutes even in the form of "answers." By rejecting questions that have only one correct solution guaranteed by using one specific procedure (Churchman 1971; Kitchener 1983; Wood 1983), we have become travelers posing questions for which there may be no final source for terminating our inquiry. Hence, we become "pilgrims" (Westerhoff 1987) with no shrine. Travelers who may or may not set course with a destination in mind. Fidelity. We've built faith, believing in our journey. We've built upon our inheritances together.

Part of my dilemma has been to decide which set of assumptions best fits my self as a researcher, a teacher. My struggle has been to integrate my beliefs about persons with all that I "inherited" about research. I'm finding the "tension" uncomfortable; perhaps my search for synthesis is unwise. Perhaps I will have to reject my inheritance and build my own fortune without the ease of past gifts. Yet, herein lies the "comfort." Within this forum I feel cared for and less afraid to set out on a new journey. I cannot make a wrong turn among those who recognize the validity, the purposefulness of questioning the truth value of alternative solutions. We travel together yet experience the journey differently. And that is okay. Ultimately our paths lead to self-understanding. And ultimately, this is the journey I envision for students in my classrooms:

a quest of thoughtful reflection, deep questioning, and caring connections. Travelers creating a sense of what it means to be a thinker, a researcher, a teacher in a world of wicked problems.

References

Berman, L. (1977). Curriculum leadership: That all may feel, value, and grow. In L. M. Berman & J. A. Roderick (Eds.), *Feeling, valuing, and the art of growing: Insights into the affective.* Washington, DC: Association for Supervision and Curriculum Development.

Berman, L. (1968). New priorities in the curriculum. Columbus, OH: Charles E. Merrill.

Churchman, C. W. (1971). *The design of inquiring systems: Basic concepts of systems and organizations.* New York: Basic Books.

Dewey, J. (1958). *Art as experience.* New York: Capicorn Books.

Gadamer, H–G. (1975). *Truth and method.* New York: Crossroad.

Heidegger, M. (1977). Holzwege. In D. F. Krell (Ed.), *Martin Heidegger: Basic Writings from Being and Time (1927) to The Task of Thinking (1964).* New York: Harper & Row, pp. 34–35.

Huebner, D. (1987). The vocation of teaching. In F. S. Bolin & J. M. Falk (Eds.), *Teacher renewal: Professional issues, personal choices.* New York: Teachers College Press.

Kitchener, K. S. (1983). Cognition, metacognition, and epistemic cognition: A three-level model of cognitive processing. *Human Development, 26,*(4) 222–32.

Lee, D. and L. Berman (1987). Teenage parents talk about school: Meanings for the curriculum. *The Educational Forum, 51*(4), 355–75.

Macdonald, J. B. and D. E. Purpel (1987). Curriculum and planning: Visions and metaphors. *Journal of Curriculum and Supervision, 2*(2), 178–92.

Noddings, N. (1986). Fidelity in teaching, teacher education, and research for teaching. *Harvard Educational Review, 56*(4), 496–510.

van Manen, M. (1984, April). *Action research as theory of the unique: From pedagogic thoughtfulness to pedagogic tactfulness.* Paper presented at the meeting of The American Educational Research Association, New Orleans, LA.

van Manen, M. (1986). *The tone of teaching.* Portsmouth, NH: Heinemann Educational Books.

van Manen, M. (Undated manuscript). "Doing" phenomenological research and writing: An introduction. Monograph No. 7, The Department of Secondary Education, The University of Alberta.

Westerhoff, J. H. (1987). The teacher as pilgrim. In F. S. Bolin & J. M. Falk (Eds.), *Teacher renewal: Professional issues, personal choices.* New York: Teachers College Press.

Wood, P. K. (1983). Inquiring systems and problem structure: Implications for cognitive development. *Human Development, 26,*(5) 249–65.

Facing the Stranger

In this second paper I speak of the stranger. Do I welcome the stranger or send the stranger away? I look to a biblical tale for guidance. I understand the message in the old text but still must respond to Ted's questioning that I am like the xenaphobe. I can only speak of a leap. It permits me to see the past somewhat differently from before. I can envision a future that I cannot fully grasp. I am aware of the height that enables me to see, where before I relied on a platform of someone else's making.

I look now and it is only now at this moment that I recognize the stranger! I feel silly. I am the stranger. No wonder I start my autobiography asking, "How will I be known?" No wonder it is the story of Abraham and Sarah that I recall. For me the story of Abraham and Sarah is a story of finding faith, a faith that becomes a way of being. To believe is to do. I've been seeking harmony between what I believe and what I do. But with this harmony of being comes awesome responsibility. For so long it was easier to hide behind the mask of anonymity provided in the positivistic tradition. Now I Must truly confront the stranger within. In doing so, I am able to commit to text words spoken in the comfort of care. I am finding faith in my ability to be.

At AERA last year I brought forth the metaphor of *quilting* to describe our being together in the group. For me, this spoke of our connectedness, our efforts to construct meaning together. Ted brought to awareness my use of the word *fingertips* in this context. *Fingertips* highlighted the importance of our written texts: our spoken words were literally transcribed into written documents. Thus it was through our fingertips that we committed the spoken word to a medium that would exist beyond the moment and eventually to a form that would engage persons beyond those present during our original dialog. The inscription of our dialog into written text gave the text autonomy. But I wasn't sure I was ready to grant the text independence.

Initially this realization generated some measure of discomfort within me. Not surprisingly, the first time the word *fingertips* appeared in my text, I referred to *fingertips* as providing an outlet for a mystical force that had entered my being. This spirit gave life to ideas that emerged at the keyboard, literally through my fingertips. I was not ready to make public my early thoughts, nor did I want to be wholly accountable for them. I was so uncertain, having so recently entered into this way of being. Had I selected the best words to give life to what was happening within me? Had I been sufficiently clear so that when the text was released readers unknown to me would be able to recreate my intentions somewhat closely? Was I ready to introduce myself to strangers? Had I disclosed too much or said too little? How would I be known?

I was inviting strangers into dialog. In the absence of my physical being, strangers would be able to re-create and reinterpret my intentions according to their own hermeneutic and experiential presuppositions, but without the promise of my reentry into the dialog (Kearney 1984). I may never know the meanings strangers find in my voice. I may never hear their voices. I was experiencing a great deal of tension. I recalled the story of Sarah and Abraham and God's injunction to welcome the stranger. Trusting their God, it was in an act of faith that Sarah and Abraham fed the three strangers and washed their tired feet. By doing so, the once barren Sarah was blessed with the ability to conceive and give life, even in her old age. Slowly, I realized by freeing my voice to text, I, like Sarah, would be able to give life. I would be able to give my words a life of their own. And like the descendants of Sarah and Abraham, as strangers entered the text, the dialog would transcend the finite horizons of the original context and become a dialog that never ends (Kearney 1984, 129).

I was finding comfort in the possibilities created by the written word, and the meaning of a hermeneutic circle was becoming personal. Persons unknown to me could inherit meaning from my written text as I have inherited meanings from others. As readers relate to the text, it would become open to a multiplicity of interpretations, becoming a springboard for making meaning. Thus meanings would be created and re-created. Most importantly, as noted by Ricoeur, persons who entered into genuine dialog with text would experience a change in his or her self-understanding and understanding of the world: "Henceforth to understand is to understand oneself in front of the text" (in Thompson 1981, 139). Differences as well as similarities in interpretations would both have an effect on the transformation of self-understanding. I was experiencing a certain transformation in my own self-understanding as I put myself in front of our texts, as I lived within the midst of our hermeneutic exchange.

As I reread the paragraphs, above, I was struck with the presence of religious overtones. In this, a paper I was preparing for AERA, have I overstepped a *boundary*? Was that the reason I have had such a horrible time coming to grips with this second presentation? I don't think so. It is not stepping over a boundary in the sense of saying the inappropriate, but rather the breaking-down of a boundary that I was experiencing and finding so difficult. Afraid to let the voice of my religious inheritance speak, I was speaking in a fragmented way, allowing only my academic inheritance voice. Thus, I was writing, refusing to engage the spiritual, and I kept rejecting the papers I had written. It wasn't until I trusted myself that my authentic voice could be given life. I let go, and that which guided my fingertips before was released. Once attuned, I was able to give voice to that which I had stifled. I found myself questioning the changes within me that freed me to speak so openly and, once freed, to commit these words to writing.

Francine speaks of a turning, Jessie a detour. I don't quite know how to speak of the changes within me. A paradigm shift, some might say, but I am inclined to say a leap, a leap of faith from the positivism I inherited within cognitive psychology toward the phenomenological tradition introduced by Husserl and Heidegger. Hermeneutics. Hermes, messenger of the gods. Maybe it was he who brought this phenomenological spirit to me. He forgot, however, to take my prior pedagogical baggage with him when he left.

The old tradition is still within me, often clamoring to be heard (especially when I'm struggling with this new and, often, difficult language.) I cannot divorce myself from the positivistic tradition I inherited. Instead, it serves as a point of departure, and I am learning to relate to it in a new way.

The term *objective* is typically used to describe the empirical tradition I inherited. The Latin root of objective means "to put against, to oppose." *Objectification* is "to cause to become an object" (Darroch and Silvers 1982, 8). Within positivism, persons participating in the research effort, both those conducting the inquiry and those who are the foci of study, as well as the resulting "texts" become things. Knowledge becomes truth "out there" and thusly conceived becomes a commodity, an object to be manipulated, owned, controlled. How appropriate that the pronoun *I* should never appear in research reports written in the positivist tradition. How fitting that persons participating in studies be labeled "subjects." How rational to enter data gleaned in this framework into a machine to be analyzed!

Somehow, I was comfortable in this tradition until I began work on my dissertation. Jessie, as a member of my committee, asked me to write to the following question: "How does your research reflect your image of persons?" I had a horrible time trying to reconcile my research methodology with my assumptions about humankind. The research question was in keeping with my assumptions, but the statistical language of control, of manipulation, of numbers replacing persons' words was not. My discomfort was heightened when I began to teach. I believed that qualities of epistemology should inform my actions as a professional, that the shape of our knowledge should become the shape of our living (Palmer 1983, 21). I could not reconcile my feelings about teaching, however, with a body of literature that alienates the knower from what is known. The tension I was experiencing related directly to the self-other dialectic so prevalent in the behavioral sciences. I needed to re-form my method of inquiry to reflect my belief that there is no knowledge set apart from the self.

I was seeking a form of research that would help me to recover my voice in inquiry as well as the voices of those sharing my inquiry. I did not awaken one day, however, and decide to leave "positivism." Rather I came to a new realm of understanding through dialog with the group, by actively engaging in an "hermeneutic undertaking" (Darroch and Silvers 1982, 10). The group set me toward thinking in a new way as we conversed informally around our dining room tables. Our conversations helped me reach a new vantage point from which I could experience horizons I had never known before as I turned inward to understand my being and to understand a world of new ideas that would someday inhabit me. Our conversations also helped me to look back at the region I was leaving with open eyes. Last year I relied upon the notion of stitching, of quilting, to describe my movement from one tradition to another. This year a leap of faith describes my movement from one tradition to another. It was the "interpretive sewing" of last year that readied me for a "leap" this year. Our dialog released me to a new way of being.

Dialog: a conversation, an interchange and discussion of ideas, especially when open and frank as in seeking mutual understanding (Merriam-Webster). *Dia-* from the Greek meaning "through or across." *Logue*: from the Greek *logus*, referring to a special kind of speaking or writing. The dialog of our group is in keeping with these roots. We speak across disciplines. Ours is a special kind of dialog, open, honest, frank, seeking understanding of others, of text, of ourselves. Oftentimes our conversations are inspirited and, for me, in-spirational. Our interpretations are not always identical. Sometimes there is overlap, sometimes not. Regardless, our voices are in harmony. We listen *carefully* like a leader of a symphony, for each section in its turn, valuing, too, the different voices as well as the silence that underscores those in sound.

Together, we also dialog with texts. Heidegger himself calls the interpretation of a traditional text a dialog, a "discourse within the tradition and with it" (cited in Marx 1985, 74). In accord with Heidegger's frame, we, as interpreters, deal not only with issues presented in the text, we each contribute our own interpretation to the subject matter of interpretation. Our reflections take us beyond the interpretation of the immediate. As stated so eloquently by Darroch and Silvers, we enter

> into an interpretive domain of communicative meaning where the signification of symbols in discourse are synthesized as meanings among equal participants who in their display of difference may enter into dialogue. (1982, 8)

Our discoveries and rediscoveries, formulations and reformulations are dynamic elements in our communicative relationship. We are a community as Jessie describes us, and it is within this caring community and in communion with these persons that I have been freed to find my voice.

References

Darroch, V. and R. J. Silvers (1982). *Interpretive human studies: An introduction to phenomenological research.* Washington, DC: University Press of America.

Kearney, R. (Ed.), (1984). *Dialogues with contemporary continental thinkers: The phenomenological heritage.* Manchester: Manchester University Press.

Krell, D. F. (Ed.) (1977). *Martin Heidegger: Basic writings from Being and Time (1927) to the Task of Thinking (1964).* New York: Harper & Row.

Marx, W. (1985). Hermeneutics and the history of being. In H. J. Silverman & D. Ihde (Eds.), *Hermeneutics and deconstruction.* Albany, New York: State University of New York Press, pp. 68–81.

Palmer, P. K. (1983). *To know as we are known/A spirituality of education.* New York: Harper & Row.

Ricoeur, P. (1984). *Dialogues with Paul Ricoeur.* In R. Kearney (Ed.), *Dialogues with contemporary thinkers: The phenomenological heritage,* Manchester: Manchester University Press, pp. 15–46.

Ricoeur, P. (1981). The hermeneutical function of distanciation. In J. B. Thompson (Ed. and Trans.), Hermeneutics and the human sciences. Cambridge: Cambridge University Press.

Thompson, J. B. (1981). *Critical hermeneutics: A study in the thought of Paul Ricoeur and Jurgen Habermas.* Cambridge: Cambridge University Press.

A Post-Symposium Conversation by Letter between Diane and Ted

(Diane participated in the AERA symposia in Washington, DC, and New Orleans. Following the latter presentation, a brief conversation with Ted led to a letter/essay she wrote three months later. Ted has titled it "Flames that Consume Not; Flames that Bring Forth." To this, Ted responded with his letter/essay titled "Being Led by the Object of Conversation." Both are presented here.)

Flames that Consume Not; Flames that Bring Forth

Dear Ted,

April seems so long ago and I have yet to share my thanks with you for your gentle questioning and provocative comments. Thus embarrassment accompanies my expression of appreciation.

As you commented at dinner in New Orleans, something profound occurred within me as I struggled to write that piece. I was trying to create a space for the emergence of a new way of being. I found myself speaking of crossing boundaries and experiencing a leap of faith. I was seeking my voice as I looked back to where I had been and as I looked forward to where I thought I wanted to be. I felt as if I had to find my authentic voice before I could sit at the "table." It is only tonight that I realize how I must proceed in my journey if I am to be able to "put myself in front of the text" and to release my text to strangers.

Since AERA, I have been struggling with some of the questions you posed. One in particular has weighed heavily on my mind. You asked how I would know when I was ready to give my words freedom from my presence; how I would know when I was ready to go from speaking to writing. You asked if I was prepared to enter the space I was trying so desperately to create. I answered, before strangers, that I was not yet ready, despite my desire to the contrary. I have tried to dig a bit deeper to understand my reluctance, my inability to let go.

In seeking to probe beneath the surface, anxieties related to such possibilities as being misrepresented or misunderstood, I recalled the story of Moses at the burning bush. While tending Jethro's flocks in the wilderness, Moses came to Horeb, the mountain of God. He saw a bush aflame yet unconsumed by the fire. God called to him out of the bush: "Moses! Moses!" He answered, "Here I am." God commanded: "Do not come closer. Remove your sandals from your feet, for the place on which you stand is holy ground. I am the God of your father, the God of Abraham, the God of Isaac, and the God of Jacob."

I wondered. Would I have seen the burning bush? Would I have heard the voices proclaiming, "I am the God of your father?" Would I have put my faith in question or would I have removed my sandals? Would I have been ready to look at God, or like Moses, would I first have turned aside?

Like this biblical figure, I have been fleeing what had been a comfortable haven. In the course of my journey, I too came upon an unfamiliar flame that did not destroy or consume what had been, but rather called upon me to question and to look closely at what was before me.

I am ready to remove my sandals. I will come to the "table" with bare feet, recognizing the "table as an altar." I will not turn away but I will look head-on into the "marvelous sight."

As I continue to journey, there will be other times that I will have to expose my bare feet to the desert sand. I realize that this is not only an act of reverence but that it is also an act of necessity. To be sufficiently sensitive to the pebbles and heat underfoot, I must remove the leather barriers that protect me from being uncomfortable. I believe, Ted, that I am ready to experience the tension that prepares one to look at things face-to-face, in ways one has never seen before. I know that such visions will lead me to seeing in new ways. I believe I am ready to continue the journey.

This letter began as an expression of gratitude for your guidance in my journey. It is comforting to have fellow wanderers willing to share roads traveled and roads to be explored. I need the companionship and more often the leadership. I am coming to grips with the solitude associated with a "detour" or a "turning," finding strength in the presence of others awaiting my return to the common path. I have found, too, that strangers, as well as known companions, can provide direction and support. There have been several good Samaritans on the roads I've journeyed. There have also been a few bandits, but I've learned I can survive their assault.

I believe I am ready to release my voice to text. Who knows? Perhaps one day, Ted, I will see not only the pattern of branches on the bonsai tree but the spaces in-between as well.

Thank you for the bridges you've created, for the paths you've cleared, and for the gentle way you help soothe scorched feet.

Sincerely,

Diane

Diane

August 11th, 1988

Dear Diane:

The sound of your voice that shimmered "in front of the text" of your recent letter/essay beckons forth our voices in conversation in New Orleans and, even earlier, in Washington, DC.

There is magic "released" in the texture of your text ("text"—that which is woven, recalling your metaphor of quilting). Dwelling as you have been in "agon" in the tensionality of the between—spatially between yourself and others (strangers); temporally between who you are and who you are not yet; between the metaphorical ground of your academic socialization and the ontological ground of your lived world—your reflective struggle must have been to some extent a jangling of discordant sounds and non-sounds, a cacophony of major and minor keys. And in spite of the presence of collegial others who open themselves to you, yet deeply within, you know it had to be your own struggle. (A helping hand that erases struggle is often no help at all.) And midst all this, a vital unfolding.

I, for one, admire you for your courage in standing *strong* face to face with your situation as you dwelt within the situation; for the open honesty in saying "I am not yet ready to let go"—an honesty without which likely you would not have been able to dwell authentically in the question that called upon you; for "putting your sayings into writing that, I feel, *turned* out to be a living in words, a vivid text." (Do you feel that you experienced moving from *expressing* thoughts in *writing* to *living* in *writing,* living in the playful quilting of words, in the being of the text as the text came into being?). My *reading* of your text, poetic as it is, indeed was an in-dwelling in the texture of your text, participating in the quilting.

At the New Orleans session your narrative on Sarah and Abraham held sway and stayed the meaning of your saying. The insightful narrative's staying power, I guess. Now in your letter/essay, your narrative on Moses and the burning bush speaks deeply; our souls are moved.

What your letter/essay allows are two questions that for me open up our understanding of the meaning of living. Lend me your ear for an "earful."

> *Question*: How shall we understand the place of tensionality within which we at times cry in tears, at other times cry with joy; we at times experience comfort, at other times experience discomfort; we at times agonize, at other times sing and dance?

When we dwell within the place of tensionality, we speak of "closing the gap," "leaping across," "bridging banks," "crossing from here to there," "stepping across."

When we speak such sayings, it seems that these sayings are made possible by the *prior* presence of two things (e.g., the positivistic world and the phenomenological world). Hence, acts like "closing the gap" seem to be a derivative act, possible because of the presence of the things a priori.

But what if we reversed our understanding, in a sense allowing the leaping or the bridging, etc., to be itself? Then we are able to ask, possibly, "What is the being of leaping? of bridging?" In so asking, could it be that we are also saying that leaping, bridging, crossing, etc., are ways of being in tension (tensionality) within which we dwell?

Here, of course, we are speaking of life and living. We recall that a violin string that is without tension is "dead" and cannot bring forth sound. A string appropriately tensioned is alive, is vibrant and resounds.

So in speaking of leaping, bridging, etc., we are speaking of a place in a range of tensionality, at the same time, seeking that which is appropriate to our human attunement. If this be so, what is it to experience discomfort or comfort? It seems to me that experiencing discomfort or experiencing comfort are ways of being in tension. And that to be in comfort is to be *standing with strength within* (tensionality (see p. 1).

It is such an image I see when I see the Chinese character for a person—not a static tensionless being but one in vivid tension in an ever-moving, ever-changing, ever-transforming world: 陰.

> (1. begins not to erase the two things (leaping from "x," leaping to "y") but to begin to erase the priority of "things" over "leaping"—the things remain but not their centrality, revealing the possibility of understanding leaping in itself;

(2. begins to diminish (not complete erasure of consuming) the instrumental character of the act of leaping or bridging, allowing us to open ourselves to the essence of leaping or bridging. It is in this sense that we come to recognize the necessity (as you put it) of removing our sandals so that pebbles can speak to the "souls" of our feet.

Recently, when I was asked to write a little piece in *Social Education,* an American social studies journal, concerning the Pacific Rim, I wrote of "Bridges that Rim the Pacific." Allow me to share my effort with you (enclosed).

Question: Dwelling within tensionality, how shall we understand the place "we left behind?"

We chatted about this before, but I feel it deserves repetition, because now, at least for me, repetition allows a new seeing, hopefully, more saliently.

When we leave a place for a new place (by leaping or by bridging), we fool ourselves by thinking we leave the old home behind. That a historic view is untenable. No matter where we roam in our journey's turnings and re-turnings, our tourings and de-tourings, historical beings that we are, we carry along with us places we've been.

So in "leaping forward," the world from which you leaped inevitably tags along in the leap.

In your essay/letter you recognize and affirm this. Yours, as I understand it, is a story not of negating the positivistic place you once called home, but rather a decentralizing of that which was once centered. It is a new tension of the string you seek, more appropriately attuned to the key you wish to live and sing within. And the comfort you now seem to be experiencing is not the experiencing of departure to a place of non-tensionality, but rather a transformation of the tensionality that allows you to stand with strength (fort) together with the situation in the situation (com). Fundamentally, we are speaking of how we live differently.

I talked too much.

Pretending I authored the letter/essay you sent me, I titled it, "Flames that consume not; flames that bring forth." ("flames" from your story of Moses; "bringing forth" from David Jardine—he was with us at the delightful luncheon in the Bourbon district—who understands "education" etymologically as "bringing forth"). I enjoyed our re-meeting and re-newed conversation, albeit by letter. And I am reminded of Gadamer who said, "We do not so much conduct a conversation as we are led by the object of our conversation."

Cordially yours,

Ted Aoki

TA/bh

Encl.

p.s. Aside from "Bridges...", I enclose a story a current student of mine attending summer sessions offered me. It speaks to "leaping."

Louise's Voice

"Whatcha doin? Can we talk?" A favorite aunt often reminds me of my questions as a young child. Given a positive response on her part, the dialog would begin.

As I reflect on growing up during World War II, I recall conversation being a major part of our lives—conversation with brothers and sister, with parents, with other relatives, and with the many persons who frequently were guests in our home. Evening meals were times of sharing what transpired during the day, arguing different perspectives, and projecting ahead as to how we might better handle similar situations another day. Guests frequently brought freshness to the conversations with tales of their lives and longings.

Following college, where I filled my program with courses focusing upon language and the human condition—the Romantic poets, Shakespeare, Chaucer, and literature from around the world, I took a detour. Taking a position in a private school teaching kindergarten part-time in order to do graduate work in English literature, I found myself so taken with the contemporary conversation of children as opposed to the historical writings of the ancients that I obtained graduate degrees in curriculum and teaching.

My experiences with children led me to the themes which have been pervasive interests—the individual as decision-maker, creativity in human relationships, and the tensions of life. Indeed my concerns probably center around the questions: What does it mean to dwell? What does it mean to inhabit the earth so that all might dwell in communities that enrich the human spirit?

Living and being in classrooms with children caused me to believe that the young can learn through dialog to

*dwell together amicably. I also learned about the won-
derful inner resources children possess—a sense of wonder, an ability to question and to search for answers, a
need to love and be loved. My more recent years in
higher education trigger questions such as: What experiences and opportunities will help those of us in colleges
and universities, both teachers and students, to gain the
understandings which make for more worthwhile living?
How can persons use their peculiarly human qualities to
live more compatibly with their fellows? What is the
place of questioning, of knowledge appropriation, and
creation in the process?*

*The brief pieces that follow focus on self as a
decision-maker, on the meaning of serving or ministering to others, and on the table as a gathering place for
meaning-making and caring. Persons whose lives are
embedded in gratitude for the gift of life and its possibilities can use conversation to share insights acquired
in solitude, to transcend the mundane and humdrum,
and to become more caring human beings.*

*At the table of our group, with my fellow travelers, I
have come to probe more deeply some of the values and
assumptions that seem to guide my being. The support,
questioning, and exchange of insights give a freshness to
being even as physical nourishment restores the physical
being.*

"Can we talk?"

Decision as Theme:
Implications for Curriculum

Our existential beings dwell in decision. Deciding to the thoughtful person is in a sense more important than learning. As a learner I may bank knowledge which may be used for present or future exchanges. As a decision-maker I enter into a deeper conversation with my being. That conversation calls me to reflect on the meaning of decisions in the context of the world in which I dwell—a world inhabited by those close at hand and those in distant places yet linked to my being.

As a professional being called to teaching, my concern with decision extends to the world of my students. I care about their being in the world. I care that together we make increasingly more sensitive decisions.

In my own thinking, writing, research, and teaching, decision-making seemed to surface. I have often tried to understand my persistent efforts to understand better the person as a decision-maker. I am not sure why the concept has such intrigue. Perhaps it is because in making decisions the person is most human. Perhaps it is because in times of uncertainty and crisis or happiness and satisfaction, individuals can possess the inner resources to determine, at least partially, how they will respond to situations. Perhaps it is because the person can always choose to continue to hope, love, learn—be alive—whatever the circumstances.

Perhaps the interest in decision arises from the assurance that persons conduct their lives in terms of what seems to make sense to them, in terms of purposes and intent, whether or not the surrounding context seems to be wholesomely integrated or hopelessly disintegrating. Even in a time when modern social thought points to the crumbling and deteriorating nature of human institutions, rules, and standards, the fact that persons can choose to think, act, and feel, frequently unwisely in the eyes of others, causes an awareness that persons are still partially the creators, sustainers, and recreators of the planet.

In considering some of the dialog of the seminar and interpretive theory in terms of decision, I decided to highlight only a few intriguing points: (1) contextual considerations, (2) tensions within the decision-maker, (3) personal qualities of the decision-maker, and (4) impediments to decision-making. Each of these points is briefly discussed in terms of themes, possible interpretation of the themes, and implications for praxis.

Contextual Considerations

Context is discussed here in terms of the context of the interpretive theory group.

What precipitated the group? An invitation was issued by one of the members to six other persons. The individuals for the most part were persons who were open, risk-takers, and in a few cases well schooled in research methodologies other than positivistic inquiry. Although initially the focus of the group was scattered, the decision was made relatively early in the life of the group to focus upon interpretive inquiry.

The members of the group had a deep interest in research. Wrote one:

> Why did I come? That is the easy question. *Research*: for me the word alone is provocative, the process is exhilarating. A forum to discuss research questions. That is what was lacking at the University of Maryland. This seemed to be a wonderful opportunity. A handful of persons with whom I could openly share my thoughts, my questions, my passion. (Diane)

Other persons expressed a similar interest in the research process. Interestingly, four of the seven members of the group (all women, though not by design), were either in dissertation stage or were new doctorates; one held the doctorate for a few years; and the other two were professors of relatively long standing. That the process of inquiry should be a binding thread among a rather diverse group of persons attests to the pervasive need of humankind to ever quest, search, and ask tough questions.

Although the emphasis upon research was the stated purpose of early meetings, as the group matured, the relationship of self to the research process, indeed the understanding of self received increasing attention. This point is discussed later in this paper.

As the group progressed, the tapes from the sessions and the occasional informal writings indicated that even as persons had persistent research interests, so they also had nagging questions as to whether to sustain membership in the group. Even such issues as what to wear, how to get to the meeting place, and whether the meetings were worth the trouble were stated as possible reasons why not to attend the monthly sessions. Yet, in spite of the complexity, the group seemed to add to already full and involved lives; it continued to meet with few absences.

In addition to the sustaining power of the research focus, the comfort, support, and stimulation of being together seemed to provide leading-on power for group members. Diane described the group as "Frustrating, Restorative, Nurturing." Throughout the sessions the sense of concern was ever evident. Refreshments were graciously served. Time was taken to hear the concerns of persons, even if they did not relate to the task at hand. The major portion of time at each session, however, was given to research issues.

The leadership of the group might provide an interesting subject of study. Originally convened by Jessie, the group seemed to look to Jessie for support and encouragement. When interpretive inquiry began to emerge as an organizing theme, leadership seemed to be shared by Francine and Jessie. Having recently completed a dissertation based upon interpretive inquiry, Francine was a rich resource. She knew the literature in the area, had conducted research using the methodology, and indeed "lived" many of the principles and tenets of interpretive inquiry. Yet, she seemed to try to wrestle with the amount of leadership to exert in the group. She wrote:

> I felt somewhat of a struggle within myself to want to engage in common reading wherein we could surface the interpretation together—Merleau Ponty and Heidegger were pronounced in my interests. I began to be fearful that we might get too preoccupied in idle talk, that is, a surface or groundless floating where we would have difficulty making the dialog our own. I began to hear an inner voice telling me I should help provide a focus or grounding, but at the same time was sensitive so as not be looked upon as expert because of my dissertation experience. I felt somewhat in limbo as to what to do or what course of action to suggest. I sought to look at my own lived experience of interpretive inquiry, and sought to enter into it more fully, but I felt like I was floating—I couldn't seem to find an anchor or common footing to approach our inquiry together. Again I had a gnawing feeling of exerting too much control. As we agreed to work on a project together for reporting at AERA that would reflect our experiences in the group, I began to feel closer to a convergence of direction. My struggle was at

this time how much I should offer the way of focus and substance. Was more being expected of me? Was I withholding too much? Why was I experiencing this struggle? Was I hesitant to be more self-revealing?

Although the struggle may have continued for Francine, the group did look to her for direction. Not all agreed entirely with the underlying premises of interpretive research, nor did they "buy into" the utilization of language of the interpretive theorists. Yet Francine continued to provide new insights, suggest readings, write the AERA proposal, and to supply the necessary structure for the group to proceed.

The AERA session served as an impetus toward an interim product.

Tensions within the Decision-Maker

An analysis of the typescripts and the informal documents prepared for the various sessions indicated that a life of decision is in a sense a dialectic—a weighing and reconciling of juxtaposed or contradictory arguments for the purpose of arriving at truth (Merriam-Webster). The root word of *choose,* an aspect of decision, means to enjoy. Thus, the tension which accompanies decision is to be enjoyed.

Considering the good humor and wit which accompanied the discussion, it appears that the individuals within the group enjoyed, at least the tensions, *to some degree,* brought about by the exercise of free will and judgment.

Among the tensions described by group members, either in papers or in sessions, were the problems of living in several worlds—of being simultaneously a mother and a college teacher. Jessie talks about "both-and." Jana described the tensions in her life in this way:

```
isolation————————group
knowing————————being
micro————————macro + micro
quantitative————————qualitative/spiritual
institution————————individual power
cynicism————————optimism
some impact————————??
```

The I-Thou dilemma so ably described by Buber (1958) was a continuing theme. A real issue centered around maintaining one's own selfhood in situations where one's own values and predispositions were not necessarily the norms of the group. On the one hand, individuals wanted to be in the mainstream of research, ideas, cutting-edge methodologies, and technical expertise. On the other hand, the predominant ethos in academic research and inquiry frequently was antithetical to one's own beliefs. How does one maintain I-ness when one needs to survive but represents a minority viewpoint? What matters? Who matters? These questions evoked much discussion. Would it be necessary to sacrifice some goods in order to obtain others? What goods should be sacrificed?

The concept of the dialectic has many implications for praxis. In what kinds of settings can the tensions generated by the multiple roles persons play be best considered? What kinds of language facilitate the issues inherent in the dialectic in which most persons abide?

In addition, many valuable questions may surface when attention is given to the tensions of life. Does attention to I-ness mean that I have no responsibility for community except where such responsibility appears to enhance my I-ness? How do faith, compassion, and interest in a larger whole influence my stance in the world?

At a practical level, consideration may be given to such questions as: When should I subordinate my own desires to the larger good? For example, consider a research issue. What qualities does a researcher have who asks a research subject to suspend his or her decision-making powers in order to participate in a research study? What would happen if there were no such studies? If such studies are conducted, how does a researcher know whether a person is truly informed?

Another practical issue relates to the dichotomy of the one and the mass. How does a state or a county or a school make requirements for schooling if the lived worlds of learners are fully considered? What would be the basis for curriculum if the lived world of the student were fully appreciated? What would be the nature of a curriculum for being? How would persons learn to live with other beings in community even as they search for meaning in their own lives?

Far more attention might be given to the tensions within the decision-maker, but to consider decision-making from another angle, considerations is now turned to certain qualities of the decision-maker.

Qualities of the Decision-Maker

Nimbleness of mind seemed to be reflected in much of the dialog of the group and written selections presented to the group. Individuals seemed to engage in many of the intellectual qualities commonly attributed to the decision-making process: seeing alternatives, predicting consequences, selecting an alternative, or living with outcomes. That individuals know some of the formalities of the process, the readily observable behaviors, is a given. That the exercise of behaviors commonly associated with decision-making takes place within a context of freedom was articulated several times. For example:

> An exhilarating freedom to be comes with that recognition of other ways of seeing, but at the same time an almost unforgivable sense of betrayal emerges from not having been given such an opportunity before. But then we go on with the newly found freedom, stumbling through on a course of self-direction, seeking that sense of interior renewal in order to accommodate and grow with that orientation one has come to value. (Francine)

At one point, a participant suggested that we should start out with what teachers *can* do, rather than with the restrictions. The need to deal with possibilities was mentioned, but one is reminded by Kierkegaard that life is actuality as well as possibility (Sontag 1979, 112).

At one meeting a number of qualities of decision-makers were captured on tape. The question was raised: "How can we help people to be more empowered themselves?" (Francine). Bringing to light the concealed, possessing faith, being energized and alive, taking risks, giving appropriate gifts—these seem to be some of the qualities of the decision-maker.

Although some references could be found to the positive qualities of decision-makers, more references were to pain, frustration, dissonance, the problem of finding self, anxiety, discomfort, loneliness, and struggle. The point was made that the individual decides when she will experience discomfort. For example, Diane indicated that pregnancy may siphon off energy so that potential intellectual discomfort may not be experienced, even though an instructor may have planned for dealing with opposing viewpoints.

Many implications for praxis can be found in dealing with or, in some instances, encouraging the qualities of the decision-maker. How do we help persons see the amount of freedom they have and to realize that they are responsible for what is done with that freedom? Many issues surface from a consideration of entry-level requirements for the university professor. How does the scholar maintain a sense of selfhood in systems which frequently have narrow but demanding claims upon the value of her life? The question is a resounding one, receiving attention both by newcomers to academia and by more seasoned persons. The topic merits attention, possibly through seminars, conferences, counseling sessions—and ultimately administrative action. Academics are being asked to "sell their souls" in some instances for the title of professor.

The mystery of much of life might be accorded more respect in academic life. What are the uncertainties rather than the certainties?

How do we prepare reasons for not knowing as well as knowing? How can persons by helped to hang on to what intuitively seems to have meaning and merit even if an explanation cannot readily be found? What can be done to enhance the valuing of creativity—a major component of decision making?

Impediments to Decision-Making

Ultimately, individuals make their own decisions regardless of circumstances. Yet institutions can serve as settings which either facilitate or deter worthwhile decisions. For example, for Diane, language, time, and the nature of research questions can be impediments to decisions. For Louise, the supremacy of the need for consistency in educational institutions can stand in the way of making new, vibrant decisions. For Francine, the giving over to the "they" can immobilize the decision-making process. Jana has pointed out that the focus on "they" can deter coming to grips with who I am and what I do. She talks about "the courage to act." The strategies of oppression are within self, according to Jana. Are the deterrents to decision basically internal? Surely constraints do make us agonize over our decisions.

What about the constraint of language? Some of our group are much more comfortable than others with the language of interpretive inquiry. Do we need to decide to use the language in order to become embedded in the dilemmas of our existence?

In praxis, the lack of attention to language, and the perceived lack of time to engage in true dialog, certainly are deterrents to decision. Persons often makes decisions "in spite of" rather than "because of." I am reminded of the case of Amy in Darroch and Silvers (1982). Young Amy's definition of "brother" had to do with the joining of two in a mutual lived experience. He "comes with you sometimes" (p. 210). Obviously, the child's concepts differed from the researcher's. Yet, how frequently dialog takes place in parallel form without pausing to recompose, to see whether each is making sense to the other.

Implications for Curriculum

The experience of the curricular inquiry group has many implications for curriculum. First and foremost, commitment to caring, communication, openness, and lack of concealment is essential. Second, the knowledge which the student shares is of significance, is worth pondering, and is worthy of being advanced farther through questions which make sense to the student rather than only the teacher. A valuing of the student and his or her knowledge is a first step to dialog, which is essential to learning to interpret at increasingly penetrating levels. An example of students and teachers collaboratively developing curriculum through dialog can be found in Douglas Barnes, *From Communication to Curriculum* (1976).

Students are not apt to benefit from curriculum development in an interpretive mode unless teachers have had the opportunity to experience personal worthwhileness and a sense that their personal knowledge is worthy of dialog. Michael Connelly and Freema Elbaz (1980) have discussed curricula based upon teachers' practical knowledge. Such curricula give credence to the fact that, ultimately, the teacher's decisions are critical in calling forth the beings of students. That teachers, therefore, consider the essence of their own beings in terms of the decisions they make seems logical.

Our knowledge is extraordinarily incomplete about what schools might be like if caring, dialog and interpretation were the norm. We do not know to what extent decisions might be different. The existential moment, however, might be richer and more vital. The curriculum might serve to help persons dwell in settings where interpretation is increasingly penetrating, and life is more satisfying.

References

Barnes, D. (1976). *From communication to curriculum.* New York: Penguin.

Buber, M. (1958). *I and thou* (2nd ed.). R. B. Smith, (Trans.). New York: Charles Scribner's Sons.

Connelly, F. M. and F. Elbaz, (1980). Conceptual bases for curriculum thought: A teacher's perspective. In A. W. Foshay (Ed.), *1980 Yearbook: Considered action for curriculum improvement.* Alexandria, VA: Association for Supervision and Curriculum Development.

Darroch, V. and R. J. Silvers (Eds.). (1982). *Interpretive human studies: An introduction to phenomenological research.* Washington, DC: University Press of America.

Sontag, F. (1979). *A Kierkegaard handbook.* Atlanta: John Knox Press.

Experiencing Teaching

*As a teacher, I can see students in a variety of ways: as ves-
sels into which knowledge is poured, as machines geared up
to utilize the knowledge developed under my tutelage, or as
total human beings with their own desires, intentions, longings, and spirit. I endeavor to view teaching as encounters of
one human being with another. When I see the others in their
"totality," I see them as sacred beings. In my being with
them, I am called upon at times to serve them, to minister
to them.*

*In searching for the meaning of "to minister," I found it
means "to dish up." Consequently I explored with doctoral
students the metaphor of "dishing up." In the process I came
to understand better the meaning of our being together on
each others' journey.*

What does it mean to be in teaching together? Are we indeed in teaching together? Or do we gather as a group of friends who enjoy each
other, who are useful to each other, and who "share a common commitment to the good?" (Bellah et al. 1985, 115). If I consider the lived
experience of a group of seven persons who for three years have
shared research dilemmas, engaged in professional and personal dialog,
been available to each other, and basked in a sense of concern one for
the other, what can be learned from the experience which helps me
better understand a major portion of my university responsibilities: assisting students as they compose doctoral dissertations? In what ways
are the informal meetings the group like and different from the experience of working with doctoral students?

In order to understand better mutuality in teaching as experienced
in the group, I want to examine it through several lenses. Then I want
to reflect on my role as a dissertation advisor. In undertaking this task,
I expect to move back and forth in time, beginning with the present.
This movement takes place partially as a result of reflecting alone, reflecting with students, and reflecting with group members. Fresh answers cause new questions. From new questions emerge different
insights.

The search for new ways to describe and more fully understand being with doctoral students began several months ago as I attempted to design my department's doctoral proposal seminar—the intent of which was for students to learn to develop a dissertation proposal within a framework of working together in critique, support, and elaboration. As the group searched for more meaningful ways for our being together in this assembly, so I was simultaneously searching for ways to make the seminar fresh, appealing, and enriching.

Thinking about being with doctoral students in their pilgrimages to their degrees, I was searching for ways of describing the experience. Faculty serve students, advise them, are available to them, and minister to them. A search for the derivation of the word *minister* indicated that it means "to dish up."

At a session of our group I shared with them what I meant by "dishing up" and added the preposition *with* after the phrase. The session was taped and transcribed. The first part of the tape included my thoughts, the latter part their reactions. Excerpts follow:

> I am trying to work with qualities of the setting where people can probe more deeply—can ask questions, can interact with others in a meaningful way on the journey to the doctorate. How does the advisor keep herself fit to engage in this type of ministry? What are the deterrents that block the advisor from being the kind of person the students need in the search for new knowledge and a new sense of being? What is that being, both of the faculty member and the student, in this journey? . . . How do we develop settings where people feel rather passionately about what they are doing—what they are engaged in? (Louise)

In my discussion with the group I raised questions about the ingredients to be mixed into the dish—giving and receiving constructive criticism, working in a community with other persons and ministering to each other on the way, becoming immersed in the task at hand, feeling the dissertation matters, taking a sabbatical from certain aspects of a crowded life, and dealing with part-timeness of student life.

I also shared with the group insights from a recently read book, *Home* (Rybczynski 1986), in which the author deals with such matters as "nostalgia," "intimacy and privacy," and "commodity and delight." The bottom line is home represents "comfort and well-being." My fundamental question at the time was: "What does it mean to have comfort in the process of dishing something up" (Louise)?

After my few minutes presentation, the group taught by raising questions, by elaborating, by searching for more apt metaphors, by suggesting readings—all done in an aura of support and comfort.

Comments from group members illustrating the above point follow:

Jessie: I'm wondering about the food business. Louise has been
             cooking up a storm. She makes all kinds of brownies.
             There it is!
Mary: You're talking about nourishment.

Discussion followed about food in classes. Jessie commented that
in her dissertation seminar, students sit around a table and share both
food and thought. The idea of a smorgasbord or a banquet was suggested by Jessie and Diane as a way of using the metaphor of food in a
large class.

The problem of the mix was discussed. Was what was being concocted in class to be bumpy or to have some lumps? Jessie commented
that every batter doesn't have to look the same. Mary suggested we
were making "stone soup."

Through the above dialog, issues pertaining to diversity of outcomes emerged. What were the outcomes of such a seminar? What
might be the expectations of different types of students? How might
being be brought forward through the writing of a dissertation?

A question was raised about my part in the mixing. I indicated that
I was mixing and dishing up *with* students.

Francine then spoke:

That notion of metaphor is interesting. Lakoff suggests that metaphor is our conceptual framework of how we look at the world.
You might want to push that further, to push all the aspects of
that metaphor. Maybe there is something you want to think about
your own sense of meaning of home. What is it in your sense of
home—as you push back to try to uncover what was significant
about that place you call home? What is it about that environment
that is relational to that environment you are trying to create in
the classroom?

Francine's question related to the meaning of home and the relation of that meaning to the classroom where doctoral students gather
has been a recurring one since the question was raised. Obviously I do
not have time to share all the thoughts that the question evoked, but
let me share a few.

When I think about home I think about Verhoeven's discussion of
an *ethos*, the root of ethics meaning "common abode" or "custom." It
is a place where people dwell which is an ethical task (1972, 140). In a
sense when I think back on my childhood home, it was a place where
the tensions and comforts of ethical decision-making seemed to imbue
our existence. It was wartime. Many dilemmas surfaced relative to living

in a nation with comparative wealth, safety, and freedom, when many were living in countries where fear abounded. New ways of living were sought in America. Our table was frequently the gathering place for sojourners, for those whose lives had been torn asunder by war's ravages. Our bedrooms frequently accommodated those who were between familiar livelihoods in an old land and new beginnings in unfamiliar places. Persons were poignantly poised between the richness of the lives they had left behind and the hope and possibility they foresaw.

The home in which they were staying was a place in which they dealt with tensions and conflicts inherent in a new situation. It was a place they left during the day and returned to in the evening as they took action to make new connections, search for jobs, and considered the linkages between their old and new lives.

In a sense, students embarking on a dissertation can be likened to those persons who have come to a new land. Feeling that the newness will bring about something better in their own lives, acting upon their hunches, and engaging in dialog to make the linkages between their inheritances and emerging thoughts and values, doctoral students need contexts in which fears can be shared as new ways of thinking and being emerge. In a sense, students and those with whom they work are taking on provisional identities (Verhoeven 1972, 140), as together faculty and students contemplate those barriers to professional and personal fulfillment and seek in as responsible ways as possible to create futures more ethically compelling for all.

In community, sharing a common "destiny" but through a struggle and communication, students and teachers take on "personalities of a higher order" (Carr 1986, 128). To engage with our students as persons is to affirm our own simultaneous need for solitude and for relatedness. Through community all have a chance to share what has been explored in solitude. Feelings of incompleteness are lessened.

The affirmation of incompleteness can cause anxiety. Francine indicated that perhaps I was "pushing the notion of comfort:"

Francine: It's interesting—our radically different focal points as far as the questions you raised. The last one—what does it mean to have comfort? You are seeking to push the notion of comfort, to help people understand. What about anxiety?

Diane: I thought of that but you were doing both.

Francine: Anxiety not in the punitive sense but to get in touch with who we are. Almost jumping in and rushing away too quickly to feel comfort, but dwelling in the anxiety until a little later.

Diane:	There are levels of anxiety that lead to growth and there're those which are debilitating. Put the comfort in with the mix.
Jessie:	I think anxiety is very high with doctoral students.
Diane:	Absolutely.

The discussion of anxiety caused me to reflect. Should the seminar basically evoke anxiety, or should it be used to help person overcome anxiety? I returned to some notes I had made in January as I was preparing for the seminar and also for our group. The group had caused me to think about some of the ideas which would probably surface in the course of the seminar. Excerpts from this paper follow:

> I have two problems with which I am dealing as I think about the course. First, students are faced with the biggest challenge of the doctoral program—a massive piece of writing. Second, they are part-time... What does it mean to be part-time? If we wholly concentrated on the task at hand, would anything be considered part-time? We could think about living totally in the moment?

Musings followed as to how dissertations could be broken down into small enough components to be manageable and at the same time make a larger whole. If we were totally committed to the task at hand, in what kinds of questions would we dwell? How does one deal with individual blocks to writing? (Becker 1986). I was concerned about the tension between a *loving* treatment of the word and a *disciplined* treatment of the word.

As I went through notes made prior to class and analyzed initial class meetings, I was aware that tension and anxiety were present. Optimal amounts? I am not sure. However, the discussion about anxiety in the group sensitized me to consider the issue in my work with students. The concern was capsulated in a statement:

> How do we see ourselves as writers? Do we have the confidence to put pen to paper or fingers to word processors? What deters confidence? Are we such an oral society that we do not value the written word? Do we value the written word too much? Does the written word seem too permanent?

Anxious questioning, puzzling—striving for some way to get a handle on the questions and possible answers (which would lead to new questions), students and faculty member struggled with the meaning of conducting research and supporting each other along the way. In the group, no one assumes the role of teacher. We teach each other. In the class, someone is designated teacher, but many of the same questions and issues surface. Perhaps in the group we gain some understanding of what students' feelings are when papers are critiqued, elaborated upon, or questioned. Perhaps we learn a little more clearly how to provide that critical tension of support and challenge so necessary for growth.

Our group was started as a support group. Our intent was to share our research. We continue to carry out the original intent, but we also have learned that relationship is a profound factor in research. Although the title we presented for the session was "Conversation across Disciplines," a better topic might have been "Conversation, Relationship, and Research."

The meaning of my doctoral seminar is that students need the freedom to explore relationship to themselves, to their worlds, to others. As students explore themselves, their attitudes, their feelings in relationship to their settings, perhaps they can free themselves to become all they are capable of becoming.

For example, one student tells of her feelings in terms of her need to have a space for writing suited to her inner life:

A ROOM WITH A VIEW: A PERSPECTIVE THAT IS

My office is a cozy spot. It is located on the ground level of our home. Two windows open up a view to a lovely, private back yard. In fact, we went to considerable expense enlarging the windows to enhance my view. To make it more accessible. But I have never been successful at writing there. I have to move all my clutter upstairs to the dining room where I first saw drab finches turn golden. A process which starts in February . . . and it is February again. The days are getting longer, house plants are growing, the earth is being renewed, and I am gaining focus. It is in the dining room where the beach plum blossoms in May and where maple leaves change colour, not fall.

My office, with beautiful mountain laurel immediately outside the window has too much filtered light. In my office I sit with sparrows scratching for food and with ground feeders who do the research a great service as they glean sustenance from gifts dropped from above. I can review tapes in my office, I can type in my office. I studied for comps there. I can sometimes even read there, but I can't think or write there.

(Maggie Neal, 1983)

Perhaps we need more focus on relationship, less on technique, more on feelings, less on logic, more on inner thoughts, less on objectivity. In any event, I think we in the group have learned to listen to each other with the intent of helping each other transcend mundaneness. Surely there are implications for our teaching.

References

Becker, H. S. (1986). *Writing for social scientists: How to start and finish your thesis, book or article.* Chicago: The University of Chicago Press.

Bellah, R. H., R. Madsen, W. M. Sullivan, A. Swidler, and S. M. Tipton (1985). *Habits of the heart: Individualism and commitment in American life.* New York: Harper & Row.

Carr, D. (1986). *Time, narrative and history.* Bloomington, IN: Indiana University Press.

Lakoff, G. and M. Johnson. (1980). *Metaphors we live by.* Chicago: The University of Chicago Press.

Rybczynski, W. (1986). *Home: A short history of an idea.* New York: Viking.

Verhoeven, C. (1972). *The philosophy of wonder:* An introduction and incitement to philosophy. M. Foran, (Trans.). New York: Macmillan.

The Table as Gathering Place

A table—what powerful and revealing exchanges may take place as persons engage in conversations around it! Even as our group has found comfort and stimulation at the table, so my memory is full of other daring, sad, and uplifting encounters at the table. Recollections of my childhood bring to the fore the significance of the table in meeting family, friends, and strangers.

As I teach I am aware of the significance of the table. It is the place, though sometimes more figuratively than literally, where students and I minister to each other—where we dish up together.

Doctoral students, who have had much of their coursework and are in the process of conducting their own research, present a special set of challenges to me. In a sense, when we teach, we minister. Last year at AERA, building on "the derivation" of *to minister,* which means "to dish up," I considered what does it mean to dish it up with doctoral students?

The idea of preparing something and dishing it up suggested to Jessie that we needed to have a table for persons to gather to enjoy what had been concocted. Our study group always gathers around a table where members as co-teachers minister to each other. Students frequently gather around a table where they as co-instructors minister to each other. The class may be a dissertation seminar, an advanced special topics course, or an informal meeting of students and teacher around a specific concern.

Three overlapping ways of thinking about the table seemed to surface: (1) the table as altar, (2) the table as gathering place, and (3) the table as bearer of what has been dished up.

Table as Altar

Buber has said,
One eats in holiness
and the table becomes an altar

(S. S. Judson, *The Quiet Eye*)

Altars evoke religious symbolism. Biblical references indicate that altars are places of sacrifice (Abraham and Isaac) or places of celebration (the passover or the last supper). The altar, too, refers to the sacred in broad terms which have been variously emphasized as "power, strength, and efficacy" (Ricoeur 1976, 60). "Within the sacred universe there are not living creatures here and there, but life is everywhere as a sacrality, which permeates everything and which is seen in the movement of the stars, the return to life of vegetation each year, and the alternation of birth and death" (p. 61). An altar reminds us of mystery, transcendence, divinity.

The table then in the context of teaching, whether it be an informal group of friends or peers engaging in formal courses of study, serves as a place where fledgling ideas are treated as sacred, where remnants of worn-out ways of being and thinking are sacrificed, and where celebration takes place as persons garner new strength and vision to accomplish the purposes they establish.

In a sense persons come to the table as pilgrims, making regular treks to a setting where they bring their past, their hopes, their visions—and hopefully find renewed strength to fulfill their callings, callings that "command" thinking (Heidegger 1962, 1977). At the table persons allow text and speech to interact with their beings. Moral convictions are firmly but "provisionally held, and in all humility is the confidence that while some illumination of the path of life has been received, doubtless more light will yet shine forth" (Phenix 1958, 290).

Transcendence or a going beyond marks the table. Attention to possibility and "radical individuation" (Heidegger 1962, 62) means that persons are seen as more than "something endowed with intelligence" (p. 74). Persons are seen in their entirety, in their essence. Education according to Huebner is the "lure of the transcendent" (1984, 114).

As the group explored various ideas relative to the transcendent and the sacred, Diane asked about the meaning of the transcendent for me as teacher. If I really allow myself to dwell in its meaning, I realize that each moment has infinite possibility, that I approach the moment with gratitude for what it might hold, and that I anticipate what might unfold in the moment. For example, I need to keep myself open to dealing with ideas which may be oblique both to student and me, to acknowledge feelings as well as insightful comments, and to deal with the dynamics that accompany the possibility of individualism within a compassionate community.

The Table as Gathering Place

As a gathering place the table provides a setting where relationships are shaped, explored, restored. In a doctoral program, those gathered at the table are sojourners traveling toward the end of their program. At the table sit the more outwardly communicative and the more intro-spective, the joyful and the anguished, the hurt and the healed. The table provides a common place where persons can affirm both their feelings of completeness and incompleteness. The table may be a place where, at times, an individual dwells alone. Whether with others or in one's own company, the table provides a place for searching one's own being and its relationship to self and fellow travelers.

The diversity at the table enriches the life of all. Huebner says, "The stranger, the alien, the enemy—anyone who is different than I am—poses an unspoken question to me, in fact to both of us. The question is why am I as I am, and why is she as she is? Her life is a possibility for me as mine is for her" (1984, 115).

The table provides opportunity for the broken, the marginal, and the clearly different. Such a mix allows for the learning of new ways of relating to others (Huebner 1985). The table allows for silence as well as speech as persons allow ideas to incubate, as they look for new meanings of their shared experiences for themselves.

So what of the teacher? Personally I struggle with many dilemmas as I sit at the table with the student. What mix of qualities do I prize? What mix does the university reward? What qualities do students seem to like in each other? What kinds of intelligence are enhanced in ad-vanced doctoral courses? What purposes do students see for their own knowing and being? How can I provide a setting in which knowing is embedded in the service of others? Am I imposing my own values on students? What kinds of diversity can the table accommodate?

The Table as Bearer of What Has Been Dished Up

The diversity of persons with their ideas causes the table to groan with possibilities. For all persons, therefore, choices have to be made. Kier-kegaard talks about the act of choosing requiring energy, seriousness, and pathos. The whole interiority of the person is involved in choice-making (Kierkegaard 1986, 177). The act of choosing is so serious that it gives a person's "nature a solemnity, a quiet worth that is never com-pletely lost" (p. 181).

Choices at the table are manifold—ideas, questions, elaborations, gaps in knowledge, inferences, support, guesses, hypotheses, theories, schools of thought, authors, journals—the list could go on. The menu for each gathering changes as those who have been dishing up try new recipes or elaborate on old ones. Persons contribute to and take from the table, sharing openly. At times those seated at the table bring a whole dish, other times one item. Whatever is at the table enriches the lives of those who partake at it.

Despite the plentitude, a focus frequently is on what is *not* on the table. A student has dealt with a question but still has not stated it in such a way that response is possible. Text cannot be found to amplify a concern. Richness yet a desire for more seems to characterize the feelings of the persons at the table. A perpetual dilemma centers around dealing with issues in their wholeness or reducing ideas to "interpreted particulars" (Polanyi 1958, 199). Royce (1964) and Phenix (1964) both see certain ways of viewing religion and philosophy as more integrative approaches to our knowing. Yet students frequently come to the table having approached their own being and its knowing in segmented fashion.

Another issue that surfaces as we sit at the table is that certain schools of thought or scholars may assume disproportionate unexamined affection. A major question surfaces as to helping students avoid the idolatrous which can negate openness (Huebner 1984, 122).

When I think about myself as the teacher at the table, I am aware that although I want to enter into the teaching act as coequal with students, nonetheless certain responsibilities fall to me. Students may or may not choose to make themselves vulnerable. They may determine the degree to which they wish to take risks in sharing their being— their hopes, joys, apprehensions, sorrows, and possibilities. Within the framework from which I work, to be authentic, I feel I must share my knowing as well as the barriers I see to knowing, my own hopes for my students as well as for myself, my own dilemmas as well as my relative certainties (if any). My approach to teaching may be disconcerting to those who view teacher primarily as a knower and the dispenser of knowledge. Ultimately I see knowledge as socially constructed.

Thus the table becomes a community of wayfarers where persons and their ideas are held as sacred, where students have opportunity to enhance their authenticity within a compassionate setting, and where all may be enriched by the feast in which they participate.

References

Heidegger, M. (1977). *Basic writings.* New York: Harper & Row.

Heidegger, M. (1962). *Being and time.* J. Macquarrie and E. Robinson, (Trans.). New York: Harper & Row.

Huebner, D. (1985). Spirituality and knowing. In E. Eisner (Ed.), *Learning and teaching the ways of knowing.* Eighty-fourth yearbook of the National Society for the Study of Education. Chicago: University of Chicago Press, pp. 159–173.

Huebner, D. (1984). The search for religious metaphors in the language of education. *Phenomenology and Pedagogy 2* (2), 112–23.

Judson, S. S. (1982). *The quiet eye: A way of looking at pictures.* Chicago: Regnery Gateway

Kierkegaard, S. S. (1986). *Either/Or: A One Volume Abridgment in a New Translation.* G. L. Stengren, (Trans.), New York: Harper & Row.

Phenix, P. (1958). *Philosophy of education.* New York: Henry Holt & Company.

Phenix, P. (1964). *Realms of meaning.* New York: McGraw-Hill.

Polanyi, M. (1958). *Personal knowledge: Towards a post-critical philosophy.* Chicago: The University of Chicago Press.

Ricoeur, P. (1976). *Interpretation theory: Discourse and the surplus of meaning.* Fort Worth: The Texas Christian University Press.

Royce, J. R. (1964). *The encapsulated man.* New York: Van Nostrand Reinhold.

Ted in Conversation with Louise

I am delighted that the upcoming *Voices of Educators* occasions this opportunity to tie another knot in the ongoing conversation you and I began more than a decade ago. I am finding that the experience of rereading your three AERA papers at one sitting is indeed a new reading, deepening my assurance that it is the claim of a call that made possible your papers: "Decision as Theme," "Experiencing Teaching," and "The Table as Gathering Place." The rereading entices me into turnings within each paper and between the papers, and I experience a deepening as the pages of the papers open me to what seems to be the fundamental question you raise: "What does it mean to inhabit the earth so that all might dwell in communication that enrich the human spirit?"

Remembering that in *Curriculum as Being* the educators are teacher educators in a university setting, you pointedly tell us of the impoverished condition of the lives of many academics in "Decision as Theme." You agonizingly say:

> Academics are being asked to "sell their souls" in some instances for the title of professor. The mystery of much of life might be accorded more respect in academic life.

Here I am reminded of Heidegger who, like you, expressed concern about how little thought is given so often to teaching. Do you recall what he said in "What calls for thinking?"

> Teaching is even more difficult than learning... Teaching is more difficult than learning because what teaching calls for is this: to let learn... If the relation between the teacher and the learners is genuine... there is never a place in it for the authority of the know-it-all or the authoritative sway of the official... It... is an exalted matter... to become a teacher—which is something else entirely than becoming a famous professor.... We must keep our eyes fixed firmly on the true relation between teacher and taught." (1977, 356).

"We must keep our eyes fixed firmly on the true relation between teacher and taught." So stressed Heidegger. I know you will agree with me that when Heidegger said, "Keep our eyes fixed firmly," he surely did not mean we should observe keenly with our naked eyes. What he meant was this: We need to think of teaching in a way we have never thought before. Thinking what? Thinking the being of the true relationship between teacher and taught. Thinking the true relation between "being" and "together." This is the question in which you dwelt when you forthrightly asked in "Experiencing Teaching" (1987 AERA): "What does it mean to be in teaching together?"

For me this question is an uncommon one. In our pedestrian everyday life as educators, we rarely if ever formulate such questions— likely because we are unable to allow such questions to come into being. I remember at the 1987 AERA session, when you and I indulged in a bit of conversation about "questioning," we chatted about the difference between "what is *teaching*?" and "What is the *experience* of teaching?" You preferred the latter, you said, because it, in allowing experience to come forth, allows us to see tension in the experience of teaching—a tension which may hold comfort and anguish simultaneously. I still remember your probing words that still resound within me:

> My feeling is I don't have to push the anguish; I've seen enough here. So the issue is to provide a setting where perhaps the anguish can come forth, making possible a new kind of being, a new way of seeing, or making visible intersections of anguish and comfort— then move forward towards new hope, new possibilities, new ways of seeing things, new ways of being. . . .

"Experiencing Teaching" indeed was on its way to being in the paper that followed, "The Table as Gathering Place," where you truly dwelt in the house of being. Your language told me so. In this house, I feel you allowed metaphors to speak, thereby deepening the meaning of the human context of engathering as teachers and taught gathered around the table. Indeed your writing reminded me of Heidegger, who speaks of the place before the hearth—a clearing wherein engather the fourfold of earth and sky, mortality and divinity—indeed a place of sanctity (Heidegger, 1977, 327–329).

Moreover, ontologically attuned, you lived in your writing, "poetically" as Heidegger would say. I liken your writing to poetic prose, very cordial as it invites readers to come to dwell with*in vita*lly. That is what I experienced when I read:

> The table . . . in the context of teaching, whether it be an informal group of friends or peers engaging in formal courses of study,

serves as a place where fledgling ideas are treated as sacred, where remnants of worn-out ways of being and thinking are sacrificed, and where celebration takes place as persons garner new strength and vision to accomplish the purposes they establish.

You wrote of your table "providing a setting where relationships are shaped, explored and restored." Your table is so different from some counters we see in kitchens where people cannot engather but just sit, not very "together," merely to eat things dished out.

But at your table where you engather, what is it, I wonder, that calls upon you and your colleagues as teachers? What calls? Do you think that in this question may reside the true meaning of the "vocation" of teaching, the true calling of what teaching is? What calls?

Shall we talk?

One further comment.

There is a thought of yours that held me for a while. You said, "I want to enter into the teaching act as coequal with students." You also said, "Certain responsibilities fall to me."

These words pull me again to the question of the relation between the teacher and the taught. Somehow, even though both teacher and taught face the unknown future together, there is, as you implied, a certain asymmetry in responsibilities. I sense a question already embedded in the above: "What indeed authorizes one to be a teacher?" I have a feeling that this question is also concerned with "What calls?"

References

Heidegger, M. (1977). What calls for Thinking? In D. F. Krell (Ed.), *Basic writings*. New York: Harper & Row.

Heidegger, M. (1977). Building, dwelling, thinking. In D. F. Krell (Ed.), *Basic writings*. New York: Harper & Row.

All Together Now:
Revisiting Themes of Our Journey

The Return of the Question:
A Point of Re-entrance

Francine

Questions can be stopped by answers... True wonderment does not ask a thousand questions. I truly wonder when the question I ask is returned to me somehow, or when it lingers and envelopes itself with a stillness, the stillness of wonder.

van Manen, *The Tone of Teaching*

The question I have been wondering about has to do with the essence of the question itself. I began my questioning of the question with a turn to Gadamer's (1975) Hermeneutic Priority of the Question as a framework for our group's inquiry throughout the year of 1986–87, in preparation for our AERA presentation that year. The form my orienting question took at that time was, "How do I enter the question?" All questions have direction, and this one was leading me down the technological path of "How-to," in search of method despite my attempts to develop a different look at questioning, as is hinted at in my concern about "entering."

The question I began with is now being returned to me as I seek a point of re-entrance through a reflection on the text of our group, and see the idea of *relationship* central in coming to understand the nature of the question. As Heidegger (1962) has suggested, in order to understand the essence of technology, we need to develop a new relationship to it, so would I now suggest that to understand the essence of the question, we also need to develop a new relationship to it. I will seek to display my "wonderings" about this insight through the opportunities created for me in the text of our group.

Reversing the Order of Question and Answer

I don't know where the questions are coming from: That's my dilemma.

> I had difficulty writing questions—I'm still back at having to write narratives to myself.
> I wrote and I don't have a single question.

What was the experience that gave rise to these reflections about questions? It was our group's attempt at pursuing Gadamer's sense of the question by trying to understand the question to which our texts were an answer. Why should this create such tension? We were, in a sense, reversing the order of our questioning by surfacing first what our texts seemed to be an answer to by locating the question the texts were asking of us as interpreters, rather than our asking of direct questions of the texts for specific answers.

We had read Gadamer's section on the Hermeneutic Priority of the Question and found his articulation of the essence of the question to be compelling in its intent, but not too lucid in how one goes about appropriating it in practice. Some of the elements we were struggling with in seeking to understand the essence of the question according to Gadamer were the following:

> It is the essence of the question to have sense, and sense involves direction.
> The emergence of the question opens up the being of the object.
> In order to be able to ask, one must want to know, which involves knowing that one does not know.
> To ask a question means to bring into the open, but the openness of the question is not boundless; it is limited by the horizon of the question.
> Because a question remains open it always includes the antithesis of yes and no—a "dialectic."
> Every sudden idea has the structure of a question, that which makes an answer possible much less than the solution to a problem.
> The art of questioning is that of being able to go on asking questions, the art of thinking (Gadamer 1975).

In bringing these ideas together in the logic of question and answer, Gadamer provides the following interpretation:

> A person who seeks to understand must question what lies behind what is said. He must understand it as an answer to a question. If we go back behind what is said, then we inevitably ask questions beyond what is said. We understand the sense of the text only by acquiring the horizon of the question. (p. 333)

Acquiring the Horizon of the Question

What does it mean to acquire the horizon of the question? As Gadamer describes it, it means learning to look beyond what is close at hand. If we have developed a relationship to questions as framed from a technical or empirical/analytic way of knowing, the horizon is near and we expect answers to resolve the questions. As I look at my attempts to establish a new relationship to questions, Mary's reflection about my geologic metaphors of knowing (referring to uncovering layers of meaning, digging deep beneath the surface) began to tug at a realization for me that my stance to questions was a deliberate attempt in seeking a new relationship to them. But what an irony. To get closer to that which is near—it was almost as if distance were being created—a pondersome digging. What is implied in this relationship of distance? Does it mean that I have to work harder to get close? When I am close to start with, do I look with too familiar a gaze? Diane seems to express that when she suggests that the "group has nudged her to go beyond the confines of her inheritance where she was valuing that which was nearest to her." But if I am working so hard to get close through my questioning, might I be pushing further away that which I seek to know? I hear Mary's words again which call for a lightening of this burdensome approach of digging to a feeling of optimism—that "what we seek in knowing is always on the verge of being known—ready to burst forth—not truly hidden but available to sight." So I think again of the task of phenomenology—to get behind that which is said, and maybe a more illuminating metaphor would be to think of Kundera's likening of a question to a knife—which offers a chance to look at what lies behind the slice. The slice is quick, but it is penetrating as an opening is created.

To create such an opening I must feel that which is being opened up. A technical question does not allow that possibility, because rather than being opened up, I experience being closed down by answers. As a group we have resisted that. As Diane suggests, "We have become travelers posing questions, for which there may be no final source for terminating our inquiry." If we consider Burch's description of questioning as "intrinsically disclosive, integrative, and invocative, with no goal beyond on-going and open ended venture of existential ontological self appropriation and self understanding" (1986, 7), Diane's observation is revealing.

Despite the initial resistance to the notion of questioning, due to the preunderstandings carried over from a technical way of knowing, we began to see how in our journey we called forth a deeper questioning of the place from which each of us were speaking. Might this have been the central question before us?—that which eluded our grasp because we were too intent on the *form* of our questioning? Drawing upon Burch again, he suggests that we do not so much posit a question, as we are encompassed by it—"we do not so much have a question as we are in it" (p. 6). How were our various voices revealed, then, by our place in the question?

What is Our Place of Dwelling When We Question?

Mary was struggling to find her place in science so she could avoid "flipping through the dense files of the filing cabinet," the metaphorical description of science which she used. As she sought to explore other ways of looking at science she described herself as "facing outward from her inheritance." There was discomfort for her with the view of science as being fragmented and not whole, but there was not denial of her relationship to it. As she faced outward, she began to see the whole—as she lived in the part she knew and by living what she knew (that which was available for sight and knowing), she began to see other possibilities. Hence, her questioning moved in the direction of the beyond—the outer realm (the leaves of her leek metaphor), giving new meaning for the inner realm (translucent core) and her place of being in it. Hopefulness is seen in her recognition of "the shifting patterns" in science which she begins to see as "capable of rupture and redesign"—a lightness of being, rather than a pondersome activity.

Jessie expresses another dimension of "turning" that moves inward through her metaphor of "detour," which she described as a "turning away from." But as she says, "Turning away from allows a turning *to* self and opportunities to contemplate." She questions whether detour might become the context for her "heart work" or the "pictures within," to which she wants to give expression. She asks, "What does it mean for me to be open to a different light?" How might that contribute to the pictures she develops within? For Jessie, the light for contemplation and "picturing" appeared to come not from a solitary dialog away from our group, but rather *with* the group as we listened to each others' stories. A powerfully telling question about that relationship is revealed in Jessie's question, "What are the questions (from the group) that help me listen to my story?"

In a struggle to determine which voice in which to speak (wanting to step away from the positivist paradigm and at the same time refusing the spiritual voice of her religious inheritance), Diane found her place in questioning by "putting herself in *front* of the text," which she describes as a "leap of faith in the movement of one tradition to another." From her hesitancy in speaking, and questioning, "How will I be known?", she takes a bold step to position herself "in front." What does such a place allow as a vantage point for seeing? For Diane, "leaping" out in front unleashed a source of "trust" that freed her up to look back on what she had been so that she could relate to it in a new way.

While not so much of a turning, but rather a heightened sense of grounding, Louise's place of questioning has been revealed in her metaphor of "Table as a Gathering Place"—where she says "one can dwell alone or in company" as one searches for one's being. She raised the question at one point: "If we were totally committed to the task at hand, in what kinds of questions would we dwell?" For her task at hand, ministering to doctoral students, the questions of her dwelling are "ethical ones" which center on the tension between provoking anxiety, and giving comfort. Deciding the balance is her living dialectic and, as she describes it, "Perhaps it is in the decision-making that a person is most human."

As we struggled with and surfaced various tensions within the group, a question by Louise was the lightening slice for me: "Do we need to decide to use the language in order to become embedded in the dilemmas of our existence?" For me, that was the place of questioning that was most freeing for seeing other possibilities and confronting my existential commitments—as I moved *from* being technologically determined *to* phenomenologically being freed, and then back with a new awakeness to the existential stirring behind my relationship to the technical.

The question that has been returned to me by reflections on our places of dwelling in our questioning is that of how we "turn" to experience the encounter questioning brings. Whether it is a "turning from," "facing outward," "a turning inward," "a leaping in front of," or "in the dialectic process of decision-making," we will "know that place for the first time" (in the words of T. S. Eliot) after we have experienced the horizons that such ways of relating call forth. Our journey is not over, and our questions linger. Stillness ... Wonder ...

Our response to such questioning concerns who we are as human beings, and it is ourselves (our having, doing, thinking, and being together) that is at the center of our questioning. We continue to "turn" in conversation and give voice to who we are as persons, teachers, and researchers, and we lend a helping hand to our being as our way traveled is questioned and thought about. With the questions that Ted raises, we have new entry points for remaining in questioning together.

References

Burch, R. (1986). Confronting technophobia: A topology. *Phenomenology + Pedagogy, 4*(2), 3–21.

Gadamer, H-G. (1975). *Truth and method.* New York: Crossroad.

Heidegger, M. (1962). *Being and time.* New York: Harper & Row.

Kundera, M. (1984). *The unbearable lightness of being.* New York: Harper & Row.

van Manen, M. (1986). *The tone of teaching.* Richmond Hill, Ontario, Canada: Scholastic.

Alienation

Mary

A sense of alienation, a disconnection from the familiar, gave the space for this group to form and grow. Were we not feeling estranged from positivistic research and technocratic education, we would not have gathered searching for other ways to think and to be. Or, had we connected to those other ways securely, we would not have worked as we have. We were in a space of both loneliness and possibility—the familiar had become strange, the strange had not yet become familiar. It was a place of possibilities, particularly those of growth and change. Ted reminded us in 1987 how, in a bonsai tree, the emptiness between the branches is as important as the branches themselves. We began in the emptiness, yet knowing there were branches for making connections and traveling on nearby.

In varying degrees we were alienated by language, that of the dominant research and educational traditions and also by the new languages—"dripping" with jargon (Francine, AERA 1987). It is hard to talk when lacking a fully familiar language: "Who can I communicate with?" asked Jessie.

Jana observed that if she used personal, everyday language of the self, then professional colleagues would not understand her language as professional, but if she used the common language of the scientific system, then she could not say what she meant. "Who can I communicate with?"

Francine and I both felt alienated as well from our subject matters. Francine wrote of her

> struggle to overcome a professional identity that has been technologically determined and the feelings of inferiority resulting from a profession that has been devalued because of its technological image.

Because home, food, and clothing are familiar to everyone, the home economist's knowledge is considered mundane and inferior; the home economist who especially knows these things is thus especially mun-

dane and inferior. Paradoxically, Francine also experiences persons saying that they were afraid to have her over for dinner because she does
know so much about food—more alienation!

I came to the group somewhat unaware of the split in my thinking.
I loved learning about the natural world in an empirical way and loved
teaching science to children, but when it came to my dissertation in
education, my own research, I unhesitatingly rejected positivism as in-
adequate and inappropriate for my question. I was doing my dissertation as the group began—group and dissertation supported each other.
Then I finished and reentered the world of teaching children and
teaching teachers about science, and the conflict became painful. What
was I doing pulling bits and pieces out of the file cabinet inheritance of
science? What about interpretation? In our group's fourth year, insight
into the metaphorical nature of all knowledge, positivistic and interpretive, knitted my thinking back together again—for now.

Another potent source of alienation for all of us is the industrial
metaphor that currently controls children's education, with its training
and testing the produce. As Jana said, we are heretics, believing

> that the person is at the center of education, not the behaviors, or
> skills, or performance.

Teaching in the grip of the industrial metaphor is fatefully restrictive
for both students and teachers.

Louise described students' deepest needs:

> Students need freedom to explore their relationships to themselves,
> to their worlds, to others [so that in exploring] perhaps they can
> free themselves to become all they are capable of becoming.

Francine had become alienated from her students in her student
teaching experience as she yielded to the school's desire to "control"
children. As she moved away from this she became less alienated from
students. In seeking her own personhood, she was drawn to that of
the students:

> To feel for others, to feel with others, it is essential that the teacher
> draw upon her own capacity for feeling. And this she can do only if
> she respects her feelings and is at home with them, feeling free to
> express them and accept them as part of herself. I learned this
> probably the hard way, fighting the struggle within myself to try to
> be more openly expressive than I was formerly capable of being.

Teaching in these dreary decades, yet believing as we do, is inher-
ently alienating. Preparing new teachers to submerge themselves is also
problematic. Regarding them as persons, how can we teach them to

regard their students objectively? Yet we must prepare them to survive in schools that demands such regard. Graduate students who are already well experienced in alienation can, however, return to the university and find that we understand.

We live in an era of widespread alienation. The connections we do make are vulnerable to rupture. Seeking to avoid alienation, we work to stay committed, not to break loose, to make our choices stick. So we stay with teaching, with home economics, with science, and with one another.

Our group of seven has become five. Alienation occurred within, even as we were banded together. The letting-goes have been painful yet necessary for all.

Jessie described the oasis that we created in the midst of alienation:

> We enjoyed and appreciated each other for what we as individuals were and not what we had done ... mostly we seemed to celebrate being together.

But she also reminded us with her meditations on the metaphor of journey that we each have our own path and solitary "heart work."

Revisiting Teaching as Journey and Detour

Jessie

Revisiting the metaphor of teaching as journey and detour began with a careful reading of our papers from the last three AERA presentations. This rereading of the group's texts was in some respects a first visit in that I now gave my whole attention to the papers in the quiet of a place far from work and home responsibilities. In this distanced setting I broke from the daily routine that had surreptitiously crowded out possibilities for genuine conversation with the deep, rich texts that I thought I had listened to and visited earlier. Now new insights on journey and detour tumbled from the texts, offering opportunities to rethink, review, reexperience, and revise my ideas. As I entertained these new perspectives, I sought new maps, new sightings, new vistas for possibilities of enriching and further developing my own text.

In discussing our group in her initial paper, Francine perceived our course as uncharted in the direction of interpretive inquiry. However, as we conversed and wrote, we began to shape an initial general mapping which later encompassed a course specification reflecting the tenets of interpretive inquiry. And in this charting, Francine saw us embarking on a search for meaning in which we confronted our individual landscapes in our formation as researchers and teachers. Although we shared some concerns, we sought our individual landscapes and pursued our personal paths on a journey that would expand our horizons. I don't think we were afraid, for we felt secure in knowing that our pilgrimage would be experienced in a context of caring.

Francine's comments on a coming out and a returning home called to mind one of Louise's views of home—home as detour. And Francine's thoughts on "shedding the conceptual shell of the empirical paradigm," an idea with which we all quite readily identified, prompted me to ask if this shedding process is both coming out and returning home.

Thus far in rereading and rethinking our papers, I have come to see journey as not necessarily requiring planning or specification beyond a commitment to finding others with whom to share and to learn something new about self alone and in community. Also, I now entertain a concept of journey that includes the coming to the journey, that the journey is always, and that it is connected to our past as well as to our present and our future. These qualities of journey invite and even make it safe for travelers to present themselves in an unfolding manner, revealing strengths, weaknesses, fears, desires, hurts, and angers. Within this frame I see our group gathered on the platform, waiting for a train we think we want to board: a train that is headed in a direction of expanding our horizons which for some may mean coming home again, for others new ports, and for still others revisiting sights in a different role or from a different perspective. The anticipation has become part of the journey. As I think about my text, this anticipation (or the before-the-embarking) seems to be implicit, but perhaps it might be made more explicit. In addition, the unplanned or serendipitous quality of journey seems to support the notion of detour as I have developed it, but I am not sure. I know that a partner helped me see detour in a new light, but I suspect that there has always been a strong desire to test the waters and that exploring detour probably gave life to that wish.

Continuing to reread our papers, I ponder Louise's remarks about the group. She speaks of the inquiry process as a binding thread among a rather diverse group of persons attesting to the need to ever quest, search, and ask tough questions. Questing, searching, asking tough questions. Could these by synonyms for journey? Reading on in Louise's paper I am moved to ask: Is mystery of life similar to detour? And finally, Louise talks about junctures when we must decide which fork to take. I do see possible connections with journey and detour, but what do we do when we meet junctures? Louise also suggests that persons sometimes feel cheated because they haven't had earlier roadmaps which might influence the decisions made at current junctures.

And so from Louise's text come new lenses revealing new perspectives and new questions for my consideration of journey and detour. The need to ever quest, to ever journey, implies that we are never not journeying. Why do I select this out of Louise's text as important to consider? And yet another question from Louise: What binds diverse persons en route? And now after the lived experience of years with the group I can ask: When and under which circumstances are the depth and intricacies of what might have appeared as tight binding revealed? Which bindings hold, tear apart, and frazzle in which circumstances, and what is the impact of these happenings on fellow travelers? Are the stretching—even the rending of the threads another example of detour as I have thought about it, and might seeing them as such help me as I try to fathom this phenomenon?

Although the mysterious in life is present more than I might wish to acknowledge, Louise's bringing it to my consciousness yet another time prompts me to ask: How might living with the concept of mystery color the pictures I create of detours? To what degree would the pictures be shrouded in mist, clouds, fog, and how might I deal with this? Would I work to dispell the mystery or would I embrace it, at least temporarily, so I could play with it a bit to see how it shades my picture and to ascertain what it conceals or reveals? Could this study of the mysterious be a detour within a detour—a place to make oneself invisible and reside where the landscape is not clear and where possibilities for creating landscapes can be unearthed? Finally, when do I feel cheated on a journey? Is it when I sense a lack of certainty, clarity, and a view of the end? But wait, aren't those just the feelings or life perspective I am trying to remove from center stage in order to make room for the mysterious and the detour which are in essence the journey? Have I come full circle, but also become richer as a result of traveling that circle? Perhaps circle is a new metaphor that can be an impetus for more reflection and for building on what I might perceive as an incomplete, gap-filled inheritance.

When Mary discusses the data problem or what we are interpreting, she quotes me as saying that what we learn is "the road you travel by to get where you went." Interesting. This is language I spoke prior to deciding on journey as a metaphor through which I might come to a better understanding of myself as teacher and collaborator. Mary builds on this idea, commenting that "the first step on our road was simple enough." I have just finished reading Jill Barklem's The High Hills, which details a journey in which mice take blankets to friends who have discovered that moths have eaten their quilts and who will not have time to make new ones before the cold settles in. After all is readied for the trip, the group embarks on the journey. Barklem begins the description of the journey with this sentence: "The first part of the journey was easy." How many and which beginnings are easy? I grew up hearing that "alle Anfänge sind schwer"—all beginnings are hard. Do I perceive beginnings as difficult? I hear myself rather consistently telling my students when they bemoan the amount and difficulty of work, "Beginnings are often difficult but things will work out if you persist."

I am now motivated to ask: Of what value is saying that all beginnings are hard or difficult? Are they really? Is this a protective strategy? Is this a strength-giving tactic? And what constitutes beginnings? Didn't the mice's journey *Begin* when they first noted a need that they could help fulfill? Again, the pre-journey which *is* the journey. I continue to question the degree to which I have dealt with this concept in my papers.

I seem to fasten on beginnings, perhaps because I sometimes tend to lose sight of them as I peer ahead, straining to see what markers announce the next turn, incline, or bridge. I wonder which beginnings seem to whisper their initial debut, and do we hear these whispers or do we let the cacophony of getting ready drown them out? Fortunately, some whispers persist and are finally heard. At other times, some whispers are never heard but function as the subconscious or unnoticed that emerges as a major force. And this leads me to think about the impact of strong silences which might also constitute beginnings and act as mainstays in some parts of our journeys. If beginnings can sort of happen as well as be heralded, one probably needs to consider the nature of contexts that invites us to hear the whispers and to welcome the silences. And we might also ask when it would be better not to listen to whispers, but at the same time, not silence them. And are there some life whispers that can never be silenced?

Perhaps paying attention to whispered or silent beginnings as well as to the more noticeable ones can be related to Mary's comments about looking through a lens narrowly or more widely. For me, at least at this point, welcoming more silent and whispered beginnings is looking through a lens more widely than before. And when I use the wider perspective, I see and create landscapes which, formerly unnoticed, now contribute to the richness of the heart pictures I create as I ponder and learn to appreciate the detours on my life journey.

Revisiting our papers has provided the rests which have permitted me to hear the following notes:

Journey as an uncharted, unfolding experience specified as travelers progress within a context of caring and of expanding horizons that can be viewed more narrowly or more broadly.

Individuals within community bound together by sometimes firm, sometimes frazzled threads of quest and searching.

Beginnings which can be felt long before they are consciously acknowledged; beginnings which *are* the journey since the journey is *always*; and beginnings which lead to junctures at which decisions made can be rich or found wanting, depending on what is perceived as necessary and important.

Detour as a coming home again; detour as dwelling in the mysterious where pictures created are shrouded in fog and darkness with only a hint of the light that is always there, even if not visible; detour as a time, place to hide, withdraw, renew.

And finally, the persistent curriculum questions: What is the nature of contexts that will make it possible for persons to see opportunities to journey characterized by these qualities? Of what value is it to make decisions about these opportunities?

Reference

Barklem, J. (1986). *The high hills.* New York: Philomel.

Caring as Being

Diane

In a short story titled "The Star Thrower," Loren Eiseley (1978) describes an early morning walk on the beach. His walk takes him past starfish gatherers and shell collectors who are busily reaping the bounty along the shoreline. Eiseley merely glances at their boiling pots. He continues his walk and moves toward a lone figure stooping in the far distance.

As Eiseley gets near, he sees that the figure is a man. Eiseley observes the man stoop and, with a quick motion, pick up and cast a stranded starfish back out into the ocean. "It may live," the man says to Eiseley. Eiseley is embarrassed. "Do you collect?" he inquires of the man. The man replies, gesturing toward the other threatened creatures of the sea lying in the sand, "Only like this. And only for the living." Eiseley stoops, carefully picks up a starfish and throws it into the water beyond the breaking surf.

To me, this is a story about care and about caring. The stranger was one who understood about nature, ecology, and life. His knowledge informed his actions which were also an expression of his passion for all things living. By exhibiting care, his behavior had leading-on power. Eiseley, too, became a "star thrower."

To me, our texts are also about care and caring. Our coming together, our continuing to work and play together for five years, is an eloquent assertion of our affection for one another. Our teaching, our research, our commitment to our professions is centered in care. And in this mode of concern and connectedness, we have together made spaces for exploring possibilities and for ways of being that we might not have known otherwise. It is these expressions of care that I found as I revisited our texts.

Caring as Affection

For many, the term *care* denotes affection, an emotional attachment, a desire to draw close. This popular interpretation was present in our texts. We became partners engaged in dialog as we turned toward one another (Mary); travelers journeying together in community yet free to detour, to turn toward ourselves so that the return was invigorated with renewal (Jessie); gatherers at a table, pilgrims who brought their past, their hopes, their visions to a place where relationships were shaped, explored, and restored (Louise); makers of relationships, values, goals, aspirations, and products—products valued for the connection they would bring to others in the receiving of that which was made in care (Francine); weavers of a quilt that no one person would own, the warp and woof of our fabric being connectedness and meaning making (Diane).

Noddings speaks of caring as "always characterized by a move away from self" (1984, 16). It is a "stepping out of one's own personal frame of reference into the other's" (p. 24). There is this kind of empathic caring exhibited in our texts. Underlying our words is a desire to go beneath the superficial and truly become involved with one another. We are truly engaged. There is a drawing together in body and spirit, and thus it is through care that each of us grew and was transformed. Through care we turn inward and outward; we enter, leave; and re-enter, we consider "the rhythm of moving back and forth between a narrower and wider framework" (Mayeroff 1971, 16). We week to experience one another fully and thus have rejected words that would reduce the "Thou to an It" (Buber 1958). We are involved with one another, and through this involvement we seek to understand the world.

Caring is not just movement toward the other, however. It is also through caring that we move toward ourselves. It is through caring that each of us is revealed and known. We write about what matters to us, what is on the edge of our knowing. We teach because we love the interaction with students, we find delight in the dialog. We research not what is "hot" and easily published, but rather that which is important to our being at the moment. As we exhibit our caring we come closer to the essence of our being, to our core. It is no wonder we speak of uncovering, of peeling back, of digging. We identify ourselves through care, and we are defined by our caring. Thus, our caring constitutes our being in the world.

This perspective of caring is akin to Heidegger's notion of persons as self-interpreting beings, that is, as persons who do not come into the world predefined but rather become defined in the course of living (1962). The focus of knowing, of being, then, occurs as we are involved in situations, not when we stand outside of situations. Care involves us in the world. Our caring created burdens as well as freedom. It was related to actuality and to potentiality. It made us vulnerable as what was once innermost and hidden became unconcealed. Caring linked us responsibly to one another, and so the stranger became an intimate. Unfortunately an intimate also became a stranger. Even at our table we experienced disconnectedness and pain. The disconnectedness was painful because we cared and yet, because we cared, we had to let go. More often, however, our caring was related to joy; joy that is an awareness of connectedness, of harmony, excitement, serenity, and the sense of being in tune with one another (Noddings 1984, 144).

Caring as Concern

Other aspects of caring were also revealed in our texts. Our caring was related to knowing, to taking charge, to watching over, to assuming responsibility. Our caring is directed toward persons, ourselves, and others, toward our research, toward the subject matter we teach. We speak eagerly, passionately, seriously. We are involved in our world in a way of being that Heidegger (1962) calls "concern." The preposition *in* is used in a way that Heidegger reserves for persons who are involved. Concern is used to describe involvement in what matters.

Heidegger speaks of two kinds of concern (1962, 158–59). First, he describes the kind of concern that "leaps in" and "takes over for the Other that with which he is to concern himself." Second, he describes the kind of solicitude that "leaps ahead" of the Other, "not in order to take away his (or her) 'care' but rather to give it back to him (or her) authentically . . . " The first kind of solicitude may create domination and dependency. The second kind of solicitude is a way of caring that empowers the other to be what he or she desires to be.

Our texts resonate with the second kind of solicitude. Our willingness to assume responsibility and to take charge were tempered by our attempts not to smother or force others into our way of seeing or being:

> Although we were united in respect to seeking a support group, it was apparent we had some different journeys in mind and different notions about how to get there . . . I found myself holding this enthusiasm in check as I sensed that maybe I was being too selfish and controlling of the group's direction . . . I had a gnawing feeling of exerting too much control. (Francine's transcript)

In these instances, our concern is ultimately about transformation. That's because our dialog, our shared reading of texts, is not a passive enterprise. Rather, our being together involves our whole selves, it forces involvement, passion, commitment, and self-reflection. Such deep involvement and concern leads to change. And change came about through questioning. Questioning was used to keep us imaginatively open to possibility and thus to expanded horizons. Our questioning was a seeking, and as such was often guided by concerns about the past, the future, and the present moment. Temporality is an important part of our concerns, of our caring.

Our concerns, the foci of what mattered, changed over time and across situations. It became clear that our past was inextricably woven with our current existence and that it propelled us toward the future as well. We each spoke of our personal history. At times, it loomed behind us, creating tension that led to turning, to detouring, to leaping, to teetering file cabinets. At other times, our history was more directly a continuation as with the gathering at tables in one another's homes. Such gathering became a pattern. It had brought comfort in the past and so became a part of the present. Indeed we plan our gathering well in advance. As we tried to live in a meaningful world, we sought new possibilities by revisiting former ways of being and by trying to understand how the past influenced the present.

This relationship of time and caring created our stories. Our present concerns were anchored in a present that was made meaningful by our past and that defines our intentions.

Caring as Action

Our caring was first revealed in our willingness to gather. We met and began to participate in a dialog of discovery. Heidegger (1962) notes that the basic meaning of *logos* is speech. Speech is to make manifest, to let something be seen, to make something accessible to another. Our first expressions of care are evident in our willingness to create relationships, to share meaningfully, to speak honestly. Our initial speaking was a powerful contribution to our coming together in community. The potency and importance of speaking is recalled in Genesis as God speaks, and through language the world comes into being. We speak and our language shapes our being in the world.

Our language exposed our caring. Caring was not merely rhetoric, however. Caring was reflected in our actions. We affirmed our caring, our concerns, our identification of what mattered in action, in relation, in involvement. Our caring was situated in our actions. This is not to say that caring created formulas or prescriptions for conditional behavior. It did not. It did, however, suggest an orientation toward the world and toward one another. There was a commitment to act on behalf of one another and to help one another grow. Mayerhoff (1971) maintains that the fundamental nature of caring for another is in helping him or her grow and actualize him- or herself.

We did experience growth. For some, this interaction with one another and with our texts was a form of personal affirmation and further confirmation. The journey in itself validated a way of being. We were, in the words of Heidegger "as wanderers on the way into the neighborhood of Being" (in Krell 1977, 224). For me, this coming together led to a transformation, to a new way of being and thinking. Thus, the caring of the others in the group had leading on power. The group became a platform, I said. Given time to reflect, however, I think it more accurate to speak of having been "thrown," as Heidegger uses the term. *Da-sein* itself occurs essentially as "thrown." It unfolds essentially in the throw of Being as the fateful sending" (in Krell 1977, 207). Looking back, the notion of leaping suggests some tacit understanding of this search for Being as a "thrown projection," a "fateful sending." In my leap of faith I was thrown into an "open region" (p. 214), thrown from "existentia" (actuality) toward "essentia" (possibility). Thus the group and our journey together created openings to possibilities; created a collective voice that heightened my awareness.

I was introduced to thinkers such as Heidegger and Gadamer and in them found a new language to express my thinking, my feeling, and eventually, my being. It is a language that "branches out and disregards all limits" (Heidegger in Krell 1977, 197). "Language is the house of Being," says Heidegger (p. 193). Action is the result of thinking, of creating with words so that thinking becomes action because it concerns the relation of Being to persons, to ideas, to nature, to things. Our actions were conceived in care.

> I picked up a star whose tube feed ventured timidly among my fingers while, like a true star, it cried soundlessly for life. I saw it with an unaccustomed clarity and cast far out. With it, I flung myself as forfeit, for the first time, into some unknown dimension of existence. (Eiseley 1978, 185)

I, too, became a star thrower.

References

Buber, M. (1958). *I and they.* Second edition. R. G. Smith, Trans. New York: Charles Scribner's Sons.

Eiseley, L. (1978). The star thrower. In L. Eiseley (Ed.), *The star thrower.* New York: Harcourt Brace Jovanovich.

Heidegger, M. (1962). *Being and time.* J. Macquarrie and E. Robinson, (Trans.), New York: Harper & Brothers.

Heidegger, M. (1977). Letter on humanism. In D. F. Krell (Ed.), *Martin Heidegger: Basic Writings from Being and Time (1927) to The Task of Thinking (1964).* New York: Harper & Row, pp. 193–242.

Krell, D. F. (Ed.) (1977). *Martin Heidegger: Basic Writings from Being and Time (1927 to The Task of Thinking (1964).* New York: Harper & Row.

Mayerhoff, M. (1971). *On caring.* New York: Harper & Row.

Noddings, N. (1984). *Caring: A feminine approach to ethics and moral education.* Berkeley: University of California Press.

Dwelling: A Return

Louise

Throughout the chapters of this book, one finds many references to dwellings. Perhaps it is as common a metaphor as journey, another fruitful metaphor for the group. Dwelling comes from a root word meaning "to tarry" or "to hesitate." In a sense we think about dwelling when we pause to consider those stopping places, those points of rest or hesitation, or those places where tarrying gives deeper insights during various phases on the journey.

Reflecting on dwelling invites a reconsideration and a reiteration of how we wrote about the metaphor. Reflecting also causes certain implications to emerge for living with those whom we call students.

Multiple Forms of Dwelling

Our group has considered dwelling in a variety of ways. Let me just share with the reader certain overlapping perspectives: (1) dwelling with self, (2) dwelling with significant others, and (3) dwelling in the larger community.

Dwelling with Self

As mentioned earlier, journey is another predominant metaphor in our thinking. In a sense, journey and dwelling may be thought of as polar ends of a continuum. Journey implies going out, dwelling suggests going in; journey involves risk-taking, dwelling implies safety; journey means reaching out, dwelling implies incorporating new insights with the old. Indeed, dwelling with the self involves taking time to rethink the ideas gathered on the journey, to search for understandings which come about as a result of the experiences of the journey, to be anguished about pieces of the puzzle of life that do not seem to fit. Jessie, in discussing Rilke's concept of "heart work," perhaps well exemplifies the meaning of dwelling with self. We do "heart work" when we allow pictures, text, feelings within us to surface and to meld them into new forms which transcend previously held ideas.

Dwelling with self involves finding the courage to explore more fully the corners, recesses, and hiding places of being. Such explorations allow persons to come to grips with themselves and that which seems to be incongruous in life. For example, Francine writes poignantly about ways of reconciling the technological priority frequently given in her chosen field with her feelings about herself. She speaks about being at peace when she made a choice to reenter her field with a perspective which incorporated a stance toward the technical. Being became the first principle. The creations of being assumed their rightful places.

Dwelling with Significant Others

Our being together seemed to evoke homey metaphors. Mary talked about peeling a leek. Diane used a quilting metaphor. We talked about cooking, about weaving, about family, about the table.

Much of the text has to do with relationship, conversation, and dialog as various members of the group sought to make meaning in safe and comfortable dwellings. Within a secure setting, persons could share doubts, uncertainties, questions, and dilemmas. The not knowing seemed to override the knowing. In other words, what was problematic, what was hurting, what were dilemmas seemed to be the topics of conversation as opposed to what was public knowledge. Persons frequently spoke of wholeness. Biblical themes emerged as *wholeness* was seen as being derived from the same root words as *holy* or *health.*

The power of dialog to enhance relationships was a theme. Also, gaps emerged in the use of language to deal with difficult situations. Language was seen as a means to uncover the concealed, but at the same time the use of it was not always adequate to handle tensions which surface in any relationship. Dwellings were seen as means of safeguarding the sacredness of life. At the same time, the struggle for better ways of being together was evident.

Dwelling in the Larger Community

What started out as a group concerned with exchanging ideas about research eventually emerged into a group concerned about the meaning of a community of educators, about the meaning of dwelling together in such a way that individuals as well as the larger group were enhanced. Our first reachings to the larger community were through presentations at such groups as the American Educational Research Association. We were learning to dwell with one another as we gathered around the tables in our respective homes. What was the meaning of dwelling in a large association with its differing perspectives?

We found that as we reached out to others, so others reached out to us. The basically human dilemmas with which we were wrestling were so much part of the human situation that for moments our dwelling appeared to be enlarged and to encompass those wishing to share in our struggles. As a pattern was developed of dwelling at tables in homes and dwelling at tables at AERA we found ourselves alternately dealing with our own discontents and discomforts and sharing the essences of our exchanges with others. As Diane has said, "We've built faith believing in our journey." Our method has been trying to live what we think. Jessie said, we give each other "enlivement, support, and courage." Perhaps as we have attempted to dwell in the larger community we have tried to establish contexts in which enlivement, support, and courage can flourish.

Implications for Schooling as Dwelling

The homey and earthy metaphors which have characterized our conversations together suggest several matters which might be considered if schooling is seen as dwelling.

First, if schools were to be seen as places where people dwell compassionately and in communion, more fundamental ways of conceiving schooling might emerge. We might think about more significant images to guide our being together, more inclusive ways of dealing with thinking, more caring ways to see that persons deal with their anxieties in comfortable settings. We might be more concerned about dealing with questions persons bring to the setting rather than providing answers to which there were no questions.

Second, we might subordinate the technocratic or the technical to the person rather than the reverse. By making computers, objectives, or the tools with which one works extensions of the person, the individual can determine how he will use a computer, if at all; how she will determine the objectives and purposes of the day; and how she will use tools in the fuller understanding of being. A student will be known by who she is rather than by what she does or makes. In brief, what we are calling for is the restoration of the person as a purposeful, meaning-making, caring being rather than an individual known by what she makes or does. Obviously making and doing are part of the human condition; but the intent, understandings, and being of the individual will play a major part in that making and doing.

Third, emanating from the above points is the notion that schools be meeting places or dwellings where relationship and communication have major importance. Students are free within the setting to create their own stories, to learn the use of symbols by using them in telling communication, to learn the arts of dialog as dwelling more deeply with self and others. Choice becomes highly significant, for persons are individuals who can learn to choose in wiser and more humane ways.

Fourth, if schooling is seen as dwelling its structure may be changed. Schools may be characterized by small classes where teachers can enter the world of students and where both have time and concern for each other. Communities are places where broken lines exist between home and school. Administrators are basically persons who dwell with teachers, enjoying more being with them than having authority over them.

In essence, much of what has characterized our group can characterize schools where students begin to learn the meaning of dwelling. Quilts were a frequent metaphor in our group. In describing the quilt Mary said, "It is stitched of the careful insights, the living experiences reflected into ideas, the weighted remark, the forgiving touch, the tolerance, the faithfulness, the moments saved and cherished... it comforts this wandering sojourner."

Our students are wandering sojourners. Schools can be dwellings where their beings are restored and regenerated. In the process students may come to know more fully the meaning of being.

Teachers, too, are wandering sojourners searching for ways to make their own lives more fulfilling as they provide meaningful settings for those whom they teach. As we have moved toward curriculum for being, we have reflected upon how we are and might be in teaching together.

For starters we feel we might

Do more listening to each other's stories,
  Develop fewer abstract generalizations,

Show more concern for the wholeness of the lives of each other,
  Be less concerned about the detachment of the total being from work,

Search for more opportunities for being together,
  Engage in less isolated teaching,

Work together more *in* teaching,
  Be less concerned about supervisory evaluation *of* teaching,

Spend more time sitting at the table dealing with particularized dilemmas,

  Spend less time thinking about prescriptions from outside the situation,

Find more ways for persons to plan to be in learning together,
  Spend less time reading texts unrelated to our central concerns,

Be more concerned about the questions,
  Be less concerned about answers to which there are no questions,

Give more attention to evolving the curriculum,
  Give less attention to "putting out guides,"

Search to understand more fully the multiple facets of the person,
  Spend less time thinking about intellect as distinct from being,

Show in diverse ways that one cares,
  Be less concerned about abstract and unexamined rules,

Give less attention to response and evaluation lacking in specifics,
  Give more attention to responsiveness within the meanings of the
  person,

Give more time to reflect on self and others as being,
  Be less concerned about persons as only linear knowers.

Postscript

We have an ethical concern related to Heidegger. In the process of our inquiry we became aware that his political affiliations and activities were incompatible with his concern for Being. We abhor his politics. We share his expressed concern for Being.

This issue confirms the value of a group such as ours which created a space for us to ponder the tensions in people's lives.